# GARDENING
# WITH HERBS

# GARDENING WITH HERBS

## A PRACTICAL GUIDE

Cathy Buchanan

THE NATIONAL TRUST

Published in Great Britain in 1999
The National Trust (Enterprises) Ltd
36 Queen Anne's Gate
London SW1H 9AS

http://bookshelf.nationaltrust.org.uk

ISBN 0 7078 0325 X

Cataloguing in Publication Data is available from the
British Library

The author and the publishers are grateful to the Garden
Picture Library for permission to reproduce the photograph
by John Glover on p.43 (*left*). All other photographs are from
the National Trust Photographic Library, and are by the
following photographers:
Stephen Robson: front cover, frontispiece, 6, 10, 11, 15, 19, 23,
26-7, 34-5, 58-9, 62, 67, 71, 91
Mike Williams: 43 (*right*)
George Wright: 50
Neil Campbell-Sharp: 70, 83, back cover
Andrew Lawson: 75

Line drawings by Jim Robins

Designed and typeset in Palatino by the
Newton Engert Partnership

Production by Louise Pope

Printed in Great Britain by Butler & Tanner Limited

FRONTISPIECE: Angelica and cardoon thrive in the hot,
dry border at Acorn Bank (see p.13).

**Publishers' Note**

The information given in this
book is not intended to be taken
as medical advice. No liability
shall attach to the author, the
contributors, or the publisher
in respect of action taken or
refrained from as a result of this
information. Any person capable
of suffering an adverse reaction
or with a condition requiring
medical attention is strongly
advised to consult a qualified
medical practitioner or suitable
therapist before using any of
the treatments referred to in
this book.

# Contents

# Introduction

What is a herb? Anyone setting out to grow, read or write about the plants we call herbs will ask this almost immediately. While compiling a book based on the herb-growing experiences of ten National Trust Head Gardeners, I continually redefined my own ideas of what a herb really is. My conclusion is generally shared by the gardeners themselves – any plant 'of use to man' can be classified as a herb, although we must gloss hastily over the occasional blurry line, such as that dividing the edible herbs from the vegetables. However even this definition seems to understate the intimacy of our relationship with herbs.

Herbs are perhaps best described as the domestic dogs of the plant world. Just as dogs were tamed by man to help in the pursuit of food, self-defence, comfort and companionship, so herbs were the plants that came out of the wild and into the gardens and homes of our ancestors knitting themselves into the fabric of everyday life. From the labourer's wife, eking out a living from the land, to the chatelaine of a castle with a huge entourage dependant on her wise management, these highly practical individuals valued the plants not just for their demonstrable benefits in diet and health, but also for the less tangible contribution they made to sweetening the quality of life in the days before freezers, household fresheners, washing machines and fabric conditioners.

Even today, modern medicine and the huge cosmetic and culinary industries have their roots firmly founded in the world of herbs. Think only of the benefits of *Digitalis* (foxglove), evening primrose and *Aloe vera* and you begin to see how much we benefit from old knowledge and careful scientific investigation into the many properties of plants.

Since herbs have played such an important role in our social history, it is particularly appropriate that the gardens of the National Trust should be custodians of many fine herb collections. At Acorn Bank in Cumbria you will find a medicinal treasure trove of familiar British native plants which thrive in our cold, damp climate. Many of these wild 'natives' such as ground elder, spearmint and nettles were actually imported by the Romans, Vikings or medieval European monastics who brought them along in much the same way as they might have brought a medicine chest. The herb garden at Buckland Abbey in Devon features many of the medicinal herbs which would have been important to the medieval monks who founded the abbey, and at Hardwick Hall, a massive herb garden recalls the heyday of herbs during Tudor times, when it was hard to name a cultivated plant for which man could find no

Golden hops in partnership with lavender in the Herb Garden at Hardwick Hall.

use at all. The twentieth-century herb garden created by Vita Sackville-West at Sissinghurst Castle, Kent, symbolises our renewed modern interest in herbs and our own folklore.

This book is not a comprehensive guide. It might be more properly described as a modest 'honest herbal', based on the experiences of the Head Gardeners in both cultivating and using the plants. The plants included are relevant to the history and design of the garden or to the lives and preferences of the Head Gardeners, among whom there are as many sceptical about the current utilitarian value of herbs as there are those who make daily use of the plants.

All of the gardeners agree with our ancestors in one way, however. So many herbs are blessed with a fine garden form, foliage colour and scent that these alone make them worth growing. The gardeners are therefore more than ready to advise on how to make the best decorative use of them, and hopefully you will find in this book a wealth of sound, practical advice.

The Plant Directory is only a starting point for herbal knowledge. It will become clear as you read that there is nothing difficult in the positioning and planting of a herb garden. It is perpetuating the plants from year to year and the detail of their cosmetic, culinary and medicinal use which makes herbs such fascinating plants to grow. Cultivation hints you should find in plenty, but in a small volume it is impossible to give more than a brief sketch of the diversity of their uses.

I am sure that each Head Gardener would hope that both their gardens and their experience will inspire readers to experiment with growing herbs in different ways and to learn much more about herbal use through the pages of compelling herbals – past and present – which the modern herb gardener has at his or her fingertips. In doing so we expand ourselves beyond the simple, satisfying physical realm of gardening and into the absorbing story of man's relationship with plants, breathing new life into the pages of our own history.

# Acorn Bank

CUMBRIA

---

Area: 1 ha (2½ acres)
Soil: Clay loam, slightly
    alkaline
Altitude: 122 m (400 ft)
Average rainfall: 914 mm (36 in)
Average climate: Very cold
    winters; warm, damp
    summers

---

During the 1960s the Herb Garden at Acorn Bank lay almost derelict. It had previously been used for vegetable production and the old seventeenth-century wall, backing onto the adjacent orchard, encases a flue heating system which may have supplied a little extra heat for peaches and apricots. The soil was therefore wonderfully fertile in this, the warmest corner, of the garden. The National Trust realised that this valuable area must be put to good use. Graham Stuart Thomas, then the Trust's Gardens Advisor, had considerable knowledge and interest in native British plants. Given the promise of the Acorn Bank site and the huge contemporary interest in medicinal and culinary herbs, he decided that this was an ideal opportunity to establish a collection of these intriguing and historically absorbing plants. Now three long borders are dedicated to the largest collection of herbal and medicinal plants in the north of England.

---

CHRIS BRAITHWAITE has been the single-handed gardener at Acorn Bank since 1982. He thinks of himself as a 'local boy', since he trained at the local agricultural college, Newton Rigg, but he comes originally from Angus in Scotland. 'Acorn Bank has always been very much a plantperson's garden and July is a good time to see the herbs here, since it is really only by the end of June that the borders begin to heave with plants. It's a very friendly, intimate garden, but can be quite spooky at dusk. I always have a feeling that someone is keeping an eye on the place. In a way it would be strange if the 'energies' of gardeners and inhabitants just disappeared completely.'

## What are herbs?

'Many people would not consider some of the plants grown here as herbal at all, in the modern, culinary sense,' Chris says. 'But traditionally herbs are simply those plants which are used by humans, particularly in the home, and they are carefully classified according to their uses. If you look through a herbal, you will see certain uses come up again and again which mostly relate to the search for cures or the easing of very basic human problems before modern medicine. You will read, for instance, that many herbs are known as 'emmenagogues' – that is they were associated with child-bearing and were used to induce labour, parturition or to control fertility.

'One of the 'Holy Grails' of the herbal past was to find a cure for syphilis, and the disease even gave its name to plants thought to be useful in its treatment – *Lobelia siphilitica*, for example. Scurvy, caused by poor diet, was another perennial problem – hence the common name 'scurvy grass' for a little British native, *Cochlearia officinalis*. We grow as many as possible of these fascinating herbs at Acorn Bank: learning about them gives a real insight into our social history.'

Broadly speaking, Chris says, herbs used to be classified into three major categories:

● **Pot herbs** These are our modern culinary herbs, which are put straight into the pot and eaten. They often include 'pot' in the name – pot marjoram (*Origanum onites*) or pot marigold (*Calendula officinalis*).

● **'Wound herbs', 'styptics' and 'simples'** These were basic home remedies. Herbs with styptic properties can staunch the flow of blood in an open wound, while a wound herb promotes healing, stimulating the re-growth of cells. Some of the best wound herbs combine both functions. The simples were the housewife's old stand-bys for easing common health problems. Betony and feverfew, for instance, were used to cure headaches.

● **Heroic cures** 'These are also medicinal,' says Chris, 'but you had to be a semi-deity to survive them! Plants such as monkshood (*Aconitum napellus*) could be taken in very small quantities to ease pain, but in large quantities they are killers. Monkshood is so powerful that I advise wearing gloves when lifting and dividing it, especially in winter when all the goodness of the plant is concentrated in the root system. If the sap gets into an open wound you may become very ill indeed.'

Monkshood

Indian physic (*Gillenia trifoliata*) enjoys the rich soil conditions of the shaded woodland border at Acorn Bank (see p.13).

## The 'truth' about herbal folklore?

Practising herbalists are usually very keen to know where their plants come from. Herbs for medicinal use were nearly always collected from the wild, because only there would the properties of the plants be relatively constant. The prescription for the actual harvest was important too, although in modern times we tend to view these recommendations as superstitious mumbo jumbo. 'Actually there is quite sound reasoning behind some of the instructions,' says Chris.

'For instance, you might be required to go out in the middle of the night, in the middle of the month, turn three times to the full moon and then harvest the herb. Turning three times is probably rubbish, but in doing this you would always be harvesting at exactly the same time of the day and month, so the chemical activity of the plant would presumably be consistent. We now know that the chemical balance of plants changes with the cycle of the moon, so the method is much smarter than it sounds.'

## Caution in using herbs

Chris believes that, although some people may meddle with plants of which they know little, the move to list poisonous plants is just as dangerous. 'We have a sign at Acorn Bank warning visitors that some of the plants are dangerous. But there are so *many* common garden plants which are poisonous, like most of the buttercup or Ranunculaceae family, including monkshood, delphiniums, clematis and buttercups themselves. And when I say dangerous I mean not just a little – the sap of some buttercups will blister your skin. Such a list could never be long enough and, if you say that some plants are dangerous, you are, *per se*, saying that the rest are 'safe'. Children should always be told to be careful with any plant,

View of the Herb Garden at Acorn Bank with black mustard and liquorice.

and you should never consume anything unless you are sure you know all about it. Plants are very powerful. Then there's the quantity in which you use something – I would guess that if you ate enough parsley, you could die! Similarly carrot juice: we've all heard about over-dosing on vitamin A.'

There are a few plants – including monkshood – of whose properties Chris feels very strongly that any keen gardener should be aware – even handling them can have quite powerful effects. Aside from the famous skin irritants such as rue foliage or hyacinth bulbs, he believes the emmenagogues may pose one of the greatest risks for the gardener unaware of their power. Two examples are rue and pennyroyal. Some shrubs such as *Daphne mezereum* can also produce quite powerful adverse reactions, but since the sap is guarded by the bark of the plant, the gardener is shielded from some of the effect.

## Herbs at Acorn Bank

Many of the herbs which flourish best in this cold, wet climate are British woodland or meadow natives which are predominantly medicinal in use. Many cosmetic or culinary herbs come from much warmer parts of the world and, although grown at Acorn Bank, are frequently less successful here than in more southerly gardens. 'Some herbs – particularly those from the Mediterranean such as thyme, lavender and sage – do better in my mother's Angus garden, hundreds of miles further north, where it tends to be cold and dry with snow during the winter – and stays that way. The plants are insulated from the worst winter wet by the snow, but even when exposed they are not fooled into early growth by the continuous changes in temperature experienced here.'

The soil in the Herb Garden at Acorn Bank is now, after centuries of improvement with both imported soil and organic matter, a light, sandy loam, sitting on a clay base, so that the plants which require more water have that as reserve deep in the soil profile. In fact a clay soil, although initially quite a struggle for herbs, actually holds great potential for achieving the ideal – dig in gravel, garden compost and well-rotted manure to improve the drainage properties with time. Improving drainage helps particularly in pulling many of the Mediterranean herbs through winter, since they would struggle to survive with root systems in wet clay for months of the year. 'Whenever I do any large-scale planting, I usually try to dig out a portion of the border completely and double-dig plenty of manure into the ground. That's not to supply nutrients to the plants, but simply to improve the soil structure. This is the only sort of 'feeding' the plants ever get, aside from mulching. If you treat plants too well, or feed them with fertilisers, you are likely to change their chemical constituents, as well as their natural habit. When growing herbs for use – whether medicinal or culinary – you should always grow organically and feed the soil, not the plant.'

## Maintaining herbs in borders

Chris believes that the key to successful gardening lies in knowing your plants and making the most of your assets to suit their individual tastes. At Acorn Bank the herb garden is divided into three long borders, each with a different regime. Most herbs at Acorn Bank are herbaceous perennials or shrubs, and the borders are treated in much the same way as any other herbaceous or mixed border.

● **The shaded, woodland border (includes shrubs like guelder rose (*Viburnum opulus*) and spindle (*Euonymus europaeus*) and herbaceous plants like Lady's mantle, self-heal, and bugle)** Of all the herbs in the garden, these woodlanders naturally enjoy the richest soil conditions, since in the wild they flourish with a continual return of nutrients to the ground as the deciduous trees above them lose their leaves in autumn. Chris mulches this border each October with a 5 cm (2 in) layer of leafmould or well-rotted farmyard manure.

● **The central, semi-shaded border (includes shrubs like holly and the apothecary's rose (*Rosa gallica* var. *officinalis*) and perennials such as mint, borage, golden marjoram and winter savory)** The central border is covered by only a very light, slightly dappled shade which is far from complete, so that many of the plants receive their share of sunlight in the course of the day. This border is less frequently mulched than the woodland border, usually on average every two or three years, tackling a small area of the border at a time when planting or replanting herbs. Not only does the mulch nourish the soil, primarily by improving the structure when it has become a little 'sad' or sour – often indicated by a surface which has sunk slightly and looks compacted – but it also protects the soil from moisture-loss while the plants are settling in. Again Chris uses leafmould or well-rotted farmyard manure.

● **The hot, dry border (includes cardoon, angelica, evening primrose, teasel, bay and aromatic Mediterranean herbs)** Chris says, 'The soil here is only mulched once in a blue moon, since it must be nutrient-poor for the health of the herbs. During the sixteen years I have been here it has been mulched as a whole perhaps only once or twice when I have noticed that the soil structure has deteriorated badly. You can only assess this through experience with your own soil and the way in which it behaves while you are digging.'

OPPOSITE: Detail of an angelica seedhead (see p.18).

## Mints for shade

*Mentha* **spp.** There are many species, hybrids and cultivars of this standard culinary herb. All produce leafy spikes of small purple to white, sage-like, hooded flowers in mid-summer and form tight mats of foliage from a rhizomatous root system which creeps at or slightly below the soil surface. The scent and flavour of each individual mint is dependant on the type and concentration of volatile oil present in the leaf. **Uses** Mint has been used as a culinary herb for centuries – there are records of mint sauce dating back to the third century! Most may be used interchangeably, according to taste. Medicinally they are valued for their antiseptic and anaesthetic properties and used as a general, soothing tonic and digestive aid.

## Cultivating mint

● Mints thrive in almost any soil in a partially or fully shaded position and may be planted or divided in autumn or spring. At Acorn Bank they grow in the semi-shaded border.

● All of the Head Gardeners experience problems in controlling the running habit of the mints. In the open border, slates inserted vertically in the soil can prevent them spreading.

● Lifting, dividing and replanting mints (**a**) in a different area of the garden each year can also curb excessive spread and helps to control mint rust which can reinfect fresh mint growth each spring from either the soil or the debris of the previous season. Chris systematically chops his clumps of mint back each season (**b**). 'To stop them running I would reduce a clump which is, say, 1 m (3 ft) across, by half. The following year, I remember which side I tackled in the previous season and hack away at the other, so that the plant has a chance to move backwards and forwards. I don't think you should try to stop them running completely. They are very hungry plants, using up the soil nutrient quickly, then wanting to move on. When I dig them up and replant them, or plant fresh clumps, I always manure the soil to keep them happy.'

● Mint rust (*Puccinia menthae*) is a fungal infection which causes distorted and yellow-flecked foliage and produces small, orange pustules on the underside of the leaf. Sometimes the plants are defoliated. Lifting, dividing and replanting in a different area of the garden each year is the best method of control, but badly affected plants should be burnt.

## Choice of mints for garden and kitchen

When selecting mints for your own garden, Chris advises that, unless you are an inveterate collector, there's little point in having more than three mints in the garden, because you

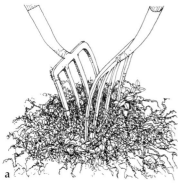

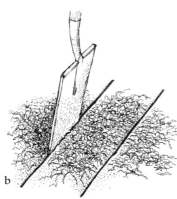

A mature clump of mint is lifted from the ground and separated using two garden forks, back to back (**a**). To curb mint's spreading habit, chop mature clumps back severely on alternate sides in successive years (**b**).

Spearmint (BOTTOM), curly
leaved spearmint (CENTRE)
and creeping pennyroyal (TOP).

are unlikely to use them. 'I'd choose Eau de Cologne mint to keep the flies away with its scent. Then I'd choose between spearmint, peppermint or apple mint for a good culinary variety. But I'd never be without Moroccan mint for my mint tea or my ice-cream, because it has the best flavour of all – quite clean and not overlaid with anything else.'

**Spearmint (*Mentha spicata*, syn. *M. viridis*)** 0·3–1m (12–36in). With light green, lance-shaped to oval, wrinkled leaves and pink or lilac flowers, this is the most common culinary mint, introduced to Britain by the Romans. Also known as 'green mint', 'pea mint', and 'lamb mint'. Susceptible to rust. 'Curly mint' (*M. spicata* 'Crispa') has very decorative, curly leaves.

**Moroccan Mint (*Mentha spicata* 'Moroccan')** 0·3–1m (12–36in). Very fresh green leaves and white flowers. Used for making the original mint teas.

**Apple Mint or Round Mint (*Mentha suaveolens*)** 0·4–1m (16–36in). Round, wrinkled, woolly leaves with a slight flavour of apples. Stems are often white-woolly and flowers pink or lilac. Good for flavouring cold drinks and resistant to rust. 'Bowles mint', a hybrid of apple mint and spearmint, which looks like a tall apple mint is said to make the best mint sauce. Variegated apple mint is a decorative cream and green-leaved variety, often called 'pineapple mint'.

**Ginger Mint (*Mentha × gracilis* 'Variegata')** 0·3–1m (12–36in). Has long, smooth, gold striped and flecked leaves, flavoured slightly of ginger. Stems sometimes slightly red-tinged with lilac flowers. Decorative, but some gardeners rate the flavour less than other mints.

**Eau de Cologne Mint, Lemon Mint (*Mentha × piperita* f. *citrata*)** 0·3–1m (12–36in). Oval, smooth, dark green, slightly lemon-flavoured leaves, tinged reddish-purple. Flowers pink-purple. Useful for drinks and pot pourri.

**Pennyroyal (*Mentha pulegium*)** 10–40cm (4–16in). A low-growing mint, much taller in flower, with round, bright green leaves and leafy spikes of purple flowers. Although primarily medicinal – for example in the treatment of depression – the main constituent of the volatile oil can cause abortion.

## Chris's favourite herbs

'We have all the major culinary herbs at home, but the ones I use most are three 'styptics': lady's mantle, self-heal and bugle', he says. 'I am always cutting myself while I'm out in the garden and I just run a tap over the cut, crush the herb leaves and wrap them round the wound. I hesitate to recommend this practice – it's probably a sure way to septicemia! – but it

Lady's Mantle (TOP) and
Self-heal (BELOW).

always works for me. Just to put you in the picture, however, my wife refuses to believe I know anything about herbs at all and thinks everything I bring home must be hemlock!'

**Lady's Mantle (*Alchemilla vulgaris*)** To 45cm (18in). With softly downy, beautifully scalloped and veined, light green leaves and a froth of lime-green flowers from June onwards, Lady's mantle is a classic foliage perennial for the herbaceous border, as well as justly popular with flower arrangers. *Alchemilla mollis* is a larger, hairier plant than *A. vulgaris* and is more frequently cultivated in gardens, although not used medicinally. Grows well in sun or partial shade on most soils, although a fertile, moisture-retentive loam suits it best. Plants should be dead-headed after flowering to prevent prolific self-sowing. Plant in autumn or spring. Divide in autumn or spring to increase or sow seed in spring. **Uses** The genus name *Alchemilla* comes from the Arabic word 'alchemy', since ancient alchemists believed that the plant had quite miraculous properties. Traditionally a wound-healing herb, it was also used to treat menstrual problems. 'This is such a good plant to have in the garden in any case,' Chris says. 'And its astringent properties stop the blood flow to a wound quite nicely, although I find it works best when the leaves are just up out of the ground in May. So you have to be very particular about when you injure yourself!'

**Self-heal (*Prunella vulgaris*)** 10-30cm (4-12in). Perennial often found wild in grassland or woodland clearings – or in your lawn! Has oval to diamond shaped leaves and erect, softly downy, flowering stalks with clusters of small, violet-purple, sage-like flowers at the tip. Larger-flowered *Prunella grandiflora* is rather more decorative and is therefore more frequently cultivated in gardens. Grows in shade or sun on almost any soil. Plant in autumn or spring. Divide in autumn or spring to increase or sow seed in spring. **Uses** Recommended as a wound herb by the herbalists John Gerard and Nicholas Culpeper in the sixteenth and seventeenth centuries and still used in modern medicine for its astringent properties, particularly for sore throats, mouth ulcers and piles.

**Bugle (*Ajuga reptans*)** 10-30cm (4-12in). Creeping perennial which grows wild in damp wood or grassland and is frequently used in gardens as a ground-covering plant for shade. Has shiny, wrinkled, oval leaves and little spikes of bright blue, sage-like flowers in early summer. 'Atropurpurea' is a good purple-bronze leaved form, while 'Multicolor' has leaves variegated cream, green and pinkish-purple. Grows in shade or partial shade on rich, moisture-retentive soils. Plant in autumn or spring. Divide in autumn or spring to increase.

**Uses** Valued for centuries as a wound herb and was also previously used for halting haemorrhage.

**Angelica (*Angelica archangelica*)** To 2m (6ft). A tall, statuesque biennial or short-lived perennial with broad, shiny, palmate leaves. The stout, hollow, fluted stems carrying dense umbrella-like heads of pale yellowish-green flowers in July betray the plant's relationship with the carrot family (Apiaceae). In the south of England prefers part-day shade on rich, moisture-retentive soil, but flourishes in the dry border at Acorn Bank. Angelica dies after setting seed, but plants generally self-sow. 'However, like many biennials such as mullein and evening primrose they often don't do this in the right place!' remarks Chris. 'If you want to transplant these self-sown seedlings into more suitable positions, you have to do this when the plants are still very small – with only one true leaf perhaps – so that you don't damage the long tap roots.' Angelica seed must be sown while still fresh and the plants pricked out into individual 9cm (3½in) pots. **Uses** Possibly best known for its hollow stems which are candied and used for decoration on puddings. In the Middle Ages it was known as *herba angelica* or 'angelic plant' reflecting the belief that it could even cure plague. Modern herbalists sometimes use angelica oil as a rub for rheumatism. Harvest angelica stems for candying in April or May.

## Tips for using herbs

- **Mint ice-cream** I find the Moroccan mint to be the most flavourful. Pick the leaves, wash them and chop them up until you have about two cupfuls of foliage. Pour boiling water over the top, stir in sugar to make a syrup and then let it all cool before adding cream or double cream in proportions of half cream to half of syrup. Then freeze – dead easy and very fresh, cooling and refreshing.

- **Mint tea** Take about 15–30g (1oz) of fresh mint and infuse in ½ litre (1pt) of boiling water. Generally a strong infusion acts as a real 'pick-me-up', while a mild infusion will have a slightly sedative effect. For a night-cap, pour 300ml (½pt) of boiling milk over a tablespoon of crushed leaves.

# Bateman's

EAST SUSSEX

Area: 2·03 ha (5 acres)
Soil: Clay, acidic
Altitude: 76 m (250 ft)
Average rainfall: 838 mm (33 in)
Average climate: Mild,
   moderate winters; warm,
   dry summers

The herb border at Bateman's has a formal design. Hedging herbs such as sage are used to create the triangular structure which is then infilled with herbs of similar growing habits.

In 1902 when Rudyard Kipling was at the pinnacle of his career, he and his wife Carrie created a peaceful, tranquil lifestyle for themselves at Bateman's. The garden was a treasured ingredient of this, and Kipling designed part of the area to the south of the house – including the Rose Garden and pond – as well as the elegant proportions of the broad Pear Alley, underplanted with a cool billow of shade-loving plants; his original drawings for the Rose Garden and pond can be seen in the house. Although there is no specific record of herb-growing at Bateman's during Kipling's day, there is more than one reference to herbs in his poems and books, and a selection of at least the most basic culinary varieties must certainly have been cultivated in his large kitchen garden.

But one can push tenuous connections too far. Just because the curry plant (*Helichrysum italicum*) carries exotic overtones of India – with which Kipling is so closely associated – this does not mean that the plant itself was a particular Kipling favourite. But for the visitor who strolls through the gates at Bateman's and immediately encounters the long herb border, that strong aroma of curry is a pungent and appropriate reminder of the house's former inhabitants.

DEREK BOBIN trained as a horticulturist with the Greater London Parks Department, before working in a private garden in Wiltshire and at the National Trust's Sheffield Park garden, East Sussex. He has been in charge at Bateman's since 1992. 'I've been gardening since I left school,' he says, 'and I've dabbled along the way in so many different aspects of horticulture. I particularly love Bateman's, because there's a bit of everything here – vegetables, fruit, cut flowers, ornamental lawn, herbaceous borders and wild garden. When I walk around the garden early on a summer's morning, I can still experience first hand the mood the Kiplings created. It's not a fussy or an overly showy garden. Just simple, restful lines, gentle planting and a deep sense of peace.'

## Herbs at Bateman's

The modern formally patterned herb border, runs along the south-east facing wall of the Kitchen Garden. It was developed during the 1980s by then Head Gardener, Alan Champion and the National Trust Gardens Advisor, Graham Stuart Thomas. The basic design – triangles of low hedging herbs like sage infilled with other herbs of compatible habit – has worked so well that there have been only minor changes.

'When you plant in this way,' comments Derek, 'it is quite important to match the vigour of the hedging herb with the 'infill' plant. The only really problematic combination here is the 'V' formed by the variegated sage, *Salvia officinalis* 'Tricolor'. It's easily the most delicate of the coloured sages and we struggle to grow it well, since it seems to detest not so much the cold, but the wet clay soil over winter. I'm afraid that it's a poor match for the vigorous soapwort.'

Even dandelion (*Taraxacum officinale*) – used in the treatment of eye disorders and urinary complaints – has a place here. 'I usually take a good deal of ribbing because I'm bothering to cultivate and label the dandelions at all! But there are no weeds in the world of the herbalist. Simply plants which have a practical use – and those which do not.'

## Tips for planting and maintaining herbs

The herbs are of great value at Bateman's simply because they are so easy to grow and produce a reliable show of foliage and flower over a very long season. 'However, the minute you begin to grow herbs in a more formal style like this, then the border becomes more labour-intensive. Not only do you have to clip them annually but, since they must look perfect at all times, their decorative lifetime is less than if you were cultivating them in a more relaxed, natural way. Individual plants of lavender, sage or santolina which make up the 'V' shapes only have a life of three years before they become too 'leggy' and ugly as formally clipped plants. If we didn't require perfection of them, that life would be extended by at least two years. The net result is that taking cuttings in late summer and growing these on is quite a chore in itself'.

'If you want to grow slightly tender things like pineapple sage, you have to take cuttings to perpetuate it. If you haven't got the time for this kind of detail, then you would be best to grow herbs in a less formal way and to forget the tender herbs and annuals which have to be planted or re-sown each spring'.

## Herbs to try

**Common Sage (*Salvia officinalis*)** 60-80cm (24-32in), with violet, pink or white flowers from June to August. Small, rather sprawling, evergreen Mediterranean shrub whose wrinkled, velvety leaves have a pungent aroma. A number of different cultivars have good leaf colour, including purple 'Purpurascens Variegata', gold and green 'Icterina' and yellow 'Kew Gold'. Try also White sage, *Salvia officinalis* 'Albiflora', with white flowers, and Spanish sage, *Salvia lavandulifolia*, a charming small shrub, with narrow, very grey leaves and bright blue flowers. Derek finds the green, cream and pink variegated cultivar called *S. officinalis* Purpurescens Group 'Tricolor' the most delicate, since it seems particularly to resent wet winter conditions. Plant sage in spring in a hot, sunny position, preferably on light, even stony, soil. May be clipped over annually in March to promote neat, bushy growth. Propagate from softwood or semi-ripe cuttings. **Uses** Both the common and botanical names derive from the Latin 'to save or cure'. Medieval tradition had it that a strong-growing sage bush indicated a prosperous household. Used for indigestion, regulating menstruation and for relieving depression, but is never given to pregnant women or epileptics. Toxic when used in excess over long periods.

*Salvia officinalis* **'Tricolor'** To overcome the problem of overwintering this sage in the open ground, Derek plans to grow his plants in 13cm (5in) pots, overwintering them in the greenhouse and then plunging them, still in their pots, into the 'V' formation each spring, spaced at the usual 22.5cm (9in) intervals. 'If it works, I shall lift them each autumn, take them out of their pots, trim the roots and the top growth – which should be a valuable source of cuttings – and repot them into fresh John Innes No. 2 compost with an added handful of grit.'

**Pineapple Sage (*Salvia elegans* 'Scarlet Pineapple')** To 1m (3ft), with spikes of red flowers in winter. Beautiful light

Pineapple Sage

green, pineapple-scented leaves and brilliant red flowers make this sub-shrubby sage particularly decorative. It may be grown in the open garden during the summer in a sunny, sheltered position on light soil, but is most frequently treated as a scented plant for a frost-free conservatory since it flowers during winter and early spring. Take softwood cuttings in summer. **Uses** The leaves may be added to fruit salads and drinks or used across a loin of pork while roasting.

## Taking softwood and semi-ripe cuttings

As the leaves of both types of cutting can rapidly lose moisture, causing them to wilt before new roots have formed, a fairly humid atmosphere is important for both, but softwood cuttings are even more vulnerable to wilt than semi-ripe cuttings.

● Non-flowering shoots make the best cuttings, but flowers may be pinched out when the cuttings are taken.

● Using a sharp knife, remove material from the shoot tips of plants – a stem length of about 10-15cm (4-6in) is usually sufficient, depending on the plant to be propagated (**a**). Put the cuttings in a plastic bag to prevent wilt before they have been prepared for insertion into the rooting medium.

● In late summer, some herbs such as sage may be propagated by a form of semi-ripe cutting known as a 'heel' cutting. In this case, the small sideshoots of the plant are simply pulled away from the main shoots with a small piece of ripened wood or 'heel' at the base.

● To prepare cuttings, cut cleanly just below a leaf joint at the base of the cutting and remove the lower leaves until there are only two or three pairs remaining at the tip (**b**). Heel cuttings should be prepared by simply trimming the 'heel' neatly and removing some of the lower leaves (**c**).

● The length of cutting will differ with each type of herb however, since the distance between leaf joints varies with species. A good rule of thumb is to allow no more than three or four pairs of leaves per cutting.

● Derek uses a good quality seed and cutting compost and prefers to insert the cuttings around the edge of a 13cm (5in) pot, setting two or three cuttings in the centre (**d**).

● He blows into a plastic bag, pulls this over the pot and secures it with an elastic band (**e**). He finds that most herb cuttings root easily on the open bench in warm weather without bottom heat. He does not normally use a hormone rooting powder.

● In very hot weather, the plastic bag can provide excessively humid conditions and may promote rot. Derek sometimes

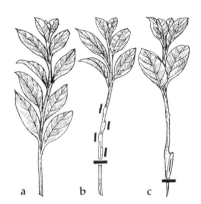

a    b    c

Preparing softwood and semi-ripe cuttings. Softwood cuttings are taken in spring and early summer when plants are growing very rapidly and therefore have a great capacity to form new roots. The entire length of each cutting is soft and is termed 'unripened' as there is no woody growth on the cutting material.

Semi-ripe cuttings are taken later in the season from shrubs such as sage. The plant material will have ripened slightly at the base and become rather woody. Semi-ripe cuttings therefore have a soft growing tip and a slightly woody base. They produce roots less rapidly than softwood cuttings, but the riper wood stores enough food to sustain the cutting for longer, increasing their chances of successful rooting during the autumn months.

Heel cuttings (**c**) are a form of semi-ripe cutting. The small sideshoots are simply pulled away from the main shoots of the plant leaving a small piece of ripened wood or 'heel' at the base.

Inserting softwood and semi-ripe cuttings.

d                              e

Close up of fennel (*Foeniculum vulgare*).

finds he has more success if he leaves them uncovered in warm weather, spraying over lightly with a hand spray first thing in the morning and then again, perhaps twice more in the course of the day, depending on the weather. Avoid spraying cuttings in strong sunlight, as the leaves may scorch.

● The polythene bag is gradually loosened and then removed completely as the cuttings root. Alternatively, slash holes in the plastic bag with a knife to wean the cutting to the less humid atmosphere outside before removing the bag completely when the cuttings are well rooted.

● Cuttings which are well-rooted in late summer are potted on immediately, usually into 9–10cm (3¹/₂–4in) pots of a loam-based, John Innes No.2 mixture. Those that root more slowly in early autumn may be left until February before potting, as poor winter light levels and lack of strong growth can cause prematurely potted cuttings to rot if over watered.

● When potted, most of the cuttings such as pineapple sage and lavender will be 'pinched' at least once to remove the growing tip to promote bushier plants. Derek finds that curry plant does not require pinching.

● Before planting out in May, Derek removes any flowers which appear on pineapple sage cuttings and feeds with a dilute liquid feed once or twice.

## Favourite herbs

'My favourite garden herbs are really those which look good in the borders at Bateman's, acting as a foil for other plants and with a scent into the bargain – santolina, fennel and curry plant are brilliant foliage herbs for any herbaceous planting.'

**Fennel (*Foeniculum vulgare*)** To 2m (6ft). A beautiful herb, smelling slightly of anise, with soft, very finely dissected feathery leaves and great umbrella-shaped heads of yellow flowers in late summer. Like other members of the Apiaceae or carrot family – including angelica and dill – it attracts hoverflies which feed on aphids, so makes a useful companion plant for the herb garden. A good, tall focal point for herb borders and the bronze ('Purpureum') or green forms are useful for colour scheming. Plant in autumn or spring in a sunny position on fertile, well-drained soil. Divide or sow seed in spring. Deadhead plants rigorously since fennel self-sows prolifically and the tap-rooted seedlings can be tricky to remove. **Uses** Medicinally fennel is credited with effective treatment of indigestion, flatulence, sore throat and eyes, bronchial congestion and urinary disorders. The dried seeds are used for stomach pain, loss of appetite and anaemia, but the oil is never given to pregnant women.

**Curry Plant (*Helichrysum italicum*)** To 60cm (24in), with yellow flowers from July to September. Derek says he has a bit of a love/hate relationship with this plant, since the strong, curry scent of the narrow grey felted leaves can be quite over-powering after rainfall. Probably best planted where you don't have to sniff it first thing in the morning if you have a delicate stomach! Plant in spring in a sunny, well-drained position. Clip in March or April if desired. Take semi-ripe cuttings in late summer. **Uses** Largely ornamental. A few chopped leaves in rice or vegetables give a mild curry flavour.

Curry Plant

## Tips for using herbs

● **Sage tea** Useful for easing coughs, sore throats and indigestion. Put 15g (¹/₂oz) of dried sage in 1 litre (2pts) of cold water and boil for five minutes, then leave to infuse for five minutes more, before straining and serving.

● **Lamb casseroled with rosemary and lavender** Rosemary is the classic herb to flavour a lamb casserole. Prepare your casserole in the normal way, but for an interesting change try taking the casserole out of the oven half an hour before the dish is completely cooked and add a sprig or two of French lavender (*Lavandula stoechas*). Highly recommended by the staff at Bateman's who advise that it is the more delicate flavouring of the French, rather than the common English, lavender which makes the difference!

● **Fennel seeds** Collect and dry fennel seeds in late summer, adding them ground to flavour lentil dishes or vegetables like brussel sprouts. May also be added to pot pourri.

# Gunby Hall

LINCOLNSHIRE

Area: 2·8ha (7 acres)
Soil: Clay loam; alkaline
Altitude: 30m (100ft)
Average rainfall: 635mm (25in)
Average climate: Cold, wet
   winters and hot, dry
   summers

The lines of the garden at Gunby Hall began to evolve from 1700 when the Massingberd family built the manor house, but it was not until the early twentieth century that Margaret Massingberd brought the garden to perfection, inspired by the design ideas of Gertrude Jekyll. Even then came a period of neglect and decline until the late 1960s when the National Trust's tenants, Mr and Mrs Wrisdale, took pity on the garden's descent into dishevelled ruin and slowly began to reclaim it, in tandem with a team of two gardeners.

The formal herb garden was designed by one of the National Trust's Gardens Advisors, Paul Miles, in the 1970s to enhance the flavour of the Edwardian garden and it uses herbs for their looks rather than their usefulness – few of the herbs now grown have a direct association with the garden's history. The aim however is to add as many different types of herbs as possible so that the visitor may gain a clear picture of the huge range of plants used by man through the centuries.

PAUL GRAY has gardened at Gunby Hall for over twenty years, becoming Head Gardener in 1980. He remembers the garden before the Wrisdales began to take its uncontrolled decline in hand. 'When I arrived here in 1975, there were just a couple of gardeners running about and keeping the grass down. We had only ten or eleven herbaceous perennials then – so tough that they were just lifted, divided and end-lessly repeated everywhere. But the excellent bones of the garden – walls and paths – were a real inspiration. All that was required was our muscle power and the will to improve on what we had. Now, for example, we've restored a good portion of the old vegetable garden to cultivation, but more than half of the original area is still laid to lawn or herbaceous plants. I've great ambitions – in spite of our limited two-man team – to dig the lawns up and come even closer to what the vegetable garden must have been in its prime.'

## Herbs at Gunby Hall

The central herb garden has a formal structure, with a basic pattern of four quarters intersected with York stone paths. The arrangement has its roots in the simple style in which medici-nal herbs and vegetables were grown in a medieval monastic garden. This kind of formal design for herbs, allowing access from a hard surface on every side of each border, has never been bettered, and it seems a particularly appropriate way in which to collect the plants which have had such an impact on our history. About a hundred different varieties are grown within the herb garden.

## Design tips for herbs

Although the position of plants may change from year to year, a number of key design elements give the herb garden a strong character and continuity.

● The borders build from low edging herbs on all four sides to a central peak provided by tall herbaceous plants with a striking form like cardoon, or evergreen shrubs like bay, myrtle and rosemary.

The Herb Garden at Gunby, showing the formal design. The stone path allows all-round access to the block beds, and the plantings rise from low shrubby herbs to tall central peaks to create the highly sculptured look.

● Herbs are planted in blocks or strips rather than individually to give a strong sculptured feeling to the planting.

● Each quarter is colour-themed with the brightest colours placed closest to the central path to attract attention.

### Herbs to try

**Comfrey, bruisewort, knitbone, boneset (*Symphytum officinale*)** 0·3–1·2m (1–4ft), flowering May to October. Perennial with drooping clusters of bell-shaped flowers in blue, purple, pink, cream or white. Both the hairy lance-shaped leaves and the thick fleshy roots are used medicinally. An invasive British native, comfrey is a useful, sometimes semi-evergreen,

ornamental herb for covering large areas of ground below trees and shrubs in a wild or woodland garden. It will grow almost anywhere, although a damp, sandy soil in part shade suits it best. Propagate by division in spring or autumn, allowing 30-60cm (12-24in) between plants. **Uses** Comfrey has been used for centuries to make compresses and poultices to treat ulcers, wounds and to help set broken bones, giving the plant its common names. The leaves and roots contain allantoin, which promotes cell proliferation and is synthesised today for use in healing creams. It also contains pyrrozolindine alkaloids, which are carcinogenic when used internally. Even the gardener who has no medicinal use for the plant will find it a valuable herb as the deep, fleshy roots are said to draw trace elements and minerals from low down in the soil profile. A liquid fertiliser, rich in potash, can be made by fermenting the foliage with water. Fresh or composted leaves may also be used as a mulch or dug into the soil. If you wish to use the foliage in this kind of vast quantity, look for the non-flowering cultivar of the Russian comfrey (*Symphytum × uplandicum*) called 'Bocking 14'. *S. caucasicum* (Caucasian comfrey) has bright blue flowers, but is more invasive than *S. officinale. S. orientale* (White comfrey) is from south-west Asia and is smaller than our native, medicinal plant. It has paler green foliage and white flowers in April and May.

**Evening Primrose (*Oenothera biennis*)** 1-1·2m (3-4ft), flowering mid-summer to autumn. The common name covers a multitude of species and subspecies from North America, but the plant most commonly grown in gardens, *O. biennis*, is a softly hairy herb with long spikes of clustered, butter-yellow flowers, which are at their perfumed best during the evening. Hardy biennial which prefers full sun and a light, sandy soil. Propagated from seed in late spring or summer, it produces a rosette of leaves during the first season, throwing up the long spike of flowers the following year. Usually perpetuates itself by self-sowing. **Uses** Oil of evening primrose is commercially extracted from the seeds of a variety of *Oenothera* species. This oil supplies an essential fatty acid (EFA) called gamma-linolenic acid (GLA), which is a precursor to many different metabolic processes affecting skin health, the immune system, wound healing, circulation and the control of inflammatory disorders. Paul says, 'Although evening primrose may be good for the skin, there is not much that you can do with the one plant in your garden. It takes millions of seeds, plus a good deal of expensive processing to produce the oil.'

## Thyme from 'Irishman's' cuttings

Thymus 'Silver Posie' and a handful of other thyme cultivars

Propagating thyme from
Irishman's cuttings.

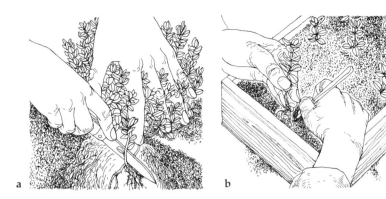

a                                          b

are more delicate and less winter-hardy than many gardeners
realise, so Paul ensures that he usually has cuttings growing
on. Marjoram and hyssop may also be propagated in this way
but are a little trickier. 'We find that the traditional soft 'tip'
cuttings of thyme taken in June or July [see Bateman's, p.22]
are so small that they are difficult to handle,' he says. 'Irishman's cuttings are less fiddly and give a higher success rate.
This method has more in common with dividing herbaceous
plants than taking a cutting, since each 'slip' has a small
portion of root still attached and grows away much faster.'

● Lift up the skirts of the mother plant still growing in the
border and pull away small shoots from the edge of the clump
below soil level. Use a sharp knife or small, narrow trowel if
necessary to ensure that you are able to cut or pull away a
portion of the root system with each shoot (**a**).

● Fill seed trays or pots with a standard seed and cutting
compost, then level and firm the surface lightly with a
'tamper' which fits the container you have used.

● Use a dibber to insert the cuttings about 2·5 cm (1 in) apart
and soak the trays using a watering can with a fine rose (**b**).
The compost should be kept just moist rather than wet after
this, thyme thrives in drier soils.

● Paul takes his cuttings of *Thymus* 'Silver Posie' in October
and November and puts the trays on the open bench in his
propagating house. Spring is just as good a time for these
cuttings however, and has the added advantage that a closed,
unheated cold frame may be used to grow the plants on.

● When the cuttings are producing new, paler-coloured top
growth you can be sure that the root system has established
well and the young plants may be potted on individually into
9 cm (3½ in) pots. If you rooted your cuttings in autumn or
late winter, it will be wise to wait until spring before potting,
as newly potted cuttings rot easily if they are overwatered in
cold, dull weather.

a

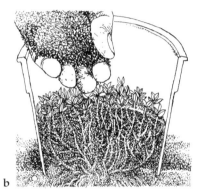

b

Layering woody-stemmed herbs.

Inserting semi-ripe cuttings
of bay around the edge of a 13cm
(5in) pot.

## Layering woody-stemmed herbs to produce new plants

'This is a good trick for plants like marjoram, winter savory, hyssop and some of the less vigorous rosemaries which you find to be slightly 'shy' to root using a normal cutting technique,' says Paul.

● In spring or early summer, take a 30cm (12in) black plastic pot and cut the base out.

● Slip the pot over the mother plant (**a**) and carefully pour a mixture of 50:50 peat and sharp sand all around the plant, leaving just the stem tips protruding (**b**).

● Keep the rooting medium damp for about three months. If you begin in April, by July most of the individual stems on the mother plant will have produced little rootlets.

● Cut the small rooted stems away from the mother plant with a sharp knife or secateurs and pot them up individually into 9cm (3½in) pots.

## Semi-ripe cuttings of bay and myrtle

'I find these evergreens easy to propagate even without heat or sophisticated propagating facilities,' Paul says.

● Prepare cuttings in the usual way (see Bateman's, p.22) in the middle of September. Myrtle and bay cuttings should both be about 12-15cm (5-6in) long.

● Insert them around the edge of a 13cm (5in) pot. This pot size takes about twelve cuttings, planted closely together.

● Place the pot in a cool, shaded area of the open garden, sheltered from wind, until about the middle of October and then transfer it to a cold frame or unheated greenhouse.

● By the middle of March the cuttings will have rooted and are ready for potting on into 9cm (3½in) pots.

● Be careful not to over-pot the young plants at any stage. Gradually pot them on, one pot size up at a time, whenever the roots have filled the pot and are showing at the base through the drainage holes.

● The plants are ready to go into the open ground when they are well-established in 14·5cm (6in) pots. Plant out in spring.

## Tips for sowing parsley

Most gardeners struggle to germinate parsley in the cold spring months, but Paul uses a surprisingly simple technique. 'Spring-sown parsley is notoriously erratic to germinate,' says Paul. 'If the seedlings dry out at all, you lose them. We sow our seed in trays in the warm months of early autumn. When they have germinated and are large enough to handle we prick out three seedlings to a 10cm (4in) pot and grow them on in the cold frames. I find that they overwinter very well and are much hardier when we plant them out in March.' Pot marigolds are treated in a similar way, but the seedlings are pricked out, twenty-four seedlings to a standard seed tray.

## Paul's favourite herbs

**Marjoram (*Origanum*)** Gardeners may be slightly confused by the different species of marjoram. For culinary use, sweet or knotted marjoram (*Origanum majorana*) has the most delicate flavour and is best added fresh to a dish just before serving, while wild or common marjoram (*Origanum vulgare*) is spicier and is often used dried in Italian tomato-based recipes. Pot marjoram (*Origanum onites*) is slightly bitter in taste, but the flavour lasts longer in cooked dishes. Several species of *Origanum* are given the common name 'oregano', but commercially even unrelated plants such *Lippia graveolens* are grown to prepare the marketed, dried herb 'oregano'. All species of *Origanum* share common properties and grow best in moisture-retentive, but sharply-drained soil in full sun. Golden marjoram (*Origanum vulgare* 'Aureum') is the exception, since the leaves may scorch in full sun – give it a position in dappled shade. **Uses** A symbol of joy for the Greeks and Romans, marjoram was planted on graves and used to crown newly-weds. Also a popular medieval strewing herb, both for its strongly aromatic leaves and antiseptic properties. Medicinally it is favoured as a sedative and aid to digestion, especially when drunk as a tea, although it should not be taken in large quantities. Good in herbal baths and pillows.

**Wild Marjoram, Oregano (*Origanum vulgare*)** 30–80cm (12–32in), flowering July to September. A creeping perennial with a woody base, forming tight mats of dark green, often purple-flushed, hairy, aromatic leaves and stiff, dark, reddish-purple stems carrying dense heads of rosy-purple flowers which attract bees and butterflies. Wild marjoram is rich in thymol which gives it its aromatic, antiseptic properties. Divide regularly in spring – on average once every four years – to maintain healthy, vigorous young plants. 'Aureum' is a very ornamental gold-leaved variant which makes a particularly pretty edging plant for dappled shade, although the yellow colouring fades as the season progresses. *O. laevigatum* is a similar, less aromatic species with dark purple-blue flowers which is only planted ornamentally; especially fine forms are 'Hopleys' and 'Herrenhausen'. Self-sows readily and makes a good herb for gravel gardens.

**Sweet or Knotted Marjoram (*Origanum majorana*)** To 25cm (10in), flowering from late July. A creeping, semi-evergreen

Sweet or Knotted Marjoram (LEFT); Wild Marjoram (RIGHT).

subshrub, with small, oval, bright green, softly hairy aromatic leaves. The tight buds of pink, pale mauve or white flowers resemble little knots, giving the plant one of its common names. Although perennial, it is normally too tender for the average frosty British winter and is generally treated as a half-hardy annual, sown in spring. Good for container cultivation in a frost-free conservatory.

**Pot or French Marjoram (*Origanum onites*)** 40–60 cm (16–24 in), flowering in August. A small, creeping, evergreen shrub from the Mediterranean, with white flowers on erect red stems and rounded, softly hairy green leaves. Less than completely hardy, and good for container cultivation. Propagate from seed in spring or by semi-ripe cuttings in late summer.

## Tips for using herbs

● 'I don't think that nationalities like the Italians who use herbs generously ever stick to a recipe as we do; they simply pick a bundle of assorted culinary herbs, chop them up and sling them in the pot. I tend to use herbs like this in risottos but I could never actually recreate the same dish twice! My favourite 'risotto' herbs are winter savory, basil, rosemary, wild marjoram and parsley.'

● After a visit to Malta in 1998 the Gray household enjoyed this recipe invented by Paul's ten-year-old daughter, Leah.

### Maltese Pasta Supreme

| | |
|---|---|
| 250 g (8 oz) wholewheat tubular pasta (try 'mezze penne rigate') | sprigs of rosemary and thyme |
| 1 tablespoon olive oil | fresh marjoram leaves, basil, parsley, chopped |
| 2 cloves of garlic | 1 glass red wine |
| 1 large onion | 50 g (2 oz) strong cheddar cheese, grated |
| 2 slices of bacon cut into strips | 1 small aubergine chopped into cubes |
| 100 g (4 oz) minced beef | freshly ground black pepper |
| 500 g (1 lb) ripe tomatoes (or a tin of plum tomatoes with juice) | |

Cook the pasta in boiling water until soft ('al dente'), then drain and leave to dry. Gently fry the garlic and onion in olive oil until soft but not burnt. Add the bacon strips and minced beef and gently stir-fry. After about five minutes, when the beef is browned, add the tomatoes, rosemary, thyme, chopped marjoram and basil and fry gently for a further ten minutes. Add the wine, cheese and aubergine, and continue to fry until the cheese has melted. Add the cooked pasta and mix well until the mixture is hot through. Remove the springs of rosemary and thyme. Season with black pepper and serve.

# Hardwick Hall

DERBYSHIRE

Area: 7ha (17½ acres)
Soil: Light, sandy loam;
    alkaline
Altitude: 198m (650ft)
Average rainfall: 660mm (26in)
Average climate: Moderate to
    cold winters; warm,
    relatively dry summers

The Countess of Shrewsbury, better known as Bess of Hardwick, built the imposing Hardwick Hall in Derbyshire in the 1590s, an enduring monument to her great spirit – and her huge wealth. The enclosed, courtyard nature of the garden, with sheltering walls and decorative gateways, is a legacy from Bess herself. However, the current structure of yew and hornbeam alleys or borders is owed to Lady Louisa Egerton, daughter of the 7th Duke of Devonshire, who spent her summer months at Hardwick until her death in 1907.

In recent years, the Trust has taken care to return to the original Elizabethan flavour and purpose of the garden, in keeping with the architecture of the Hall itself and the lifestyle of its creator. The new 1960s Herb Garden, one of the largest in England, is perhaps the triumphant pinnacle of this endeavour, with its vast array of the herbs and edible crops which were so essential in maintaining the life and health of the household who inhabited Elizabethan Hardwick Hall.

ROBIN ALLAN trained at the Royal Botanic Gardens, Edinburgh, and worked both in commercial horticulture and private gardens before arriving to lead the staff of three at Hardwick Hall in 1983. 'My original interest in plants years ago was in the native flora of Britain', he says, 'and when I first began to work, it was a question of diversifying and trying to translate that into a career.' It seems particularly appropriate that he should now care for one of the largest collections of herbs in England. His interest in botany and the more scientific aspects of horticulture now finds one expression when he puts National Trust Careership students through their paces, teaching them the skills of 'plantsmanship' which is the real hallmark of the dedicated gardener – amateur or professional. As a result, his office is always decked with plants in jars – including many herbs – the remnants of the 'plant idents' to which trainees are treated on a weekly basis!

## Herbs at Hardwick Hall

There is very little hard evidence for an Elizabethan herb garden at Hardwick Hall but, as Robin emphasises, 'Bess was a very self-sufficient woman and there is no reason to doubt that she would have considered a 'Physick' or herb garden as important as her own bakery and forge, since herbs were valued perhaps more highly by the Elizabethans than at any time, before or since'. The Hall houses a series of thirty octagonal needlework panels depicting herbs, commissioned

OVERLEAF: Golden hop pyramids add height to the Herb Garden at Hardwick Hall.

by Bess, and experts believe that the most advanced herbal of her day, Pietro Andrea Mattioli's volumes (published in 1568 and 1572), may have served as a reference for the work.

Today's herb garden was designed by Paul Miles, the Trust Gardens Advisor who also produced plans for Gunby Hall. It uses a traditional quartered design – with borders bounded on all sides by paths – in a style which could have been used for herb plantings in the days of Bess.

Robin has found that the design is deceptively simple. 'It was only when we began to move plants about that I realised how much careful thought had gone into the original plan. But move the plants we must, since few herbs – in particular the sage or Lamiaceae family – will enjoy staying in the same place for long. I think they are naturally 'ramblers', always moving on to new soil when they have exhausted the old. The system of blocks and rows actually provides us with a ready-made pattern for rotation, although planning it – if you think that we must have thirty members of Lamiaceae in here just for starters – is quite complex.'

## Design tips for herbs

● **Formal herb walk** For a sophisticated pathway choose three or four herbs with complementary foliage and form, and repeat for a very structured, 'designer' look. At Hardwick the two main sides of the herb garden are divided by a broad central path and the Assistant Head Gardener, Philip Astley, dreamed up an imaginative plan using the shapes of dark green bay, neat, blue-leaved rue (*Ruta graveolens* 'Jackman's Blue') and the spiky foliage of the orris root (*Iris germanica* var. *florentina*) planted in sequence to spill over and soften the paved edge. The visual effect is splendid, although Robin warns, 'Rue can cause blisters when it is touched by those with sensitive skins, particularly in warm weather.'

● **Height with herbs** Try using climbing edible or medicinal plants such as runner beans, hops or even honeysuckle grown on wooden 'wigwams' to add height to a herb border. The herb garden at Hardwick Hall is potentially a vast, rather flat area, so wigwams carrying a crop of runner beans were incorporated into the original design at crucial corner sites. There are four 4m (12ft) larch poles used to make each one of the thirty-two wigwams and these are driven into the soil to a depth of 80–90cm (2½–3ft) so that a total of about 3m (9·8ft) is available for climbing plant support. The runner beans have now been replaced with golden and green hops (*Humulus lupulus* 'Aureus' and *H. lupulus*). One hop grows in the centre of each wigwam, and after a little early-season persuasion to twirl around their supports they are left to their own devices.

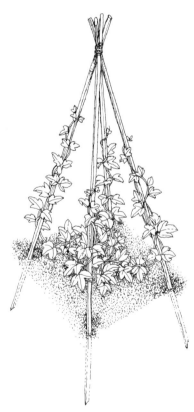

Training hops up a wigwam support to add height to the herb border.

Since hops are herbaceous, the dead top growth must be cut back and removed at the end of each season. 'The hedgehogs love them too – that tangled mass is a favourite place for them to set up house!' comments Robin. Hops are best treated with caution by sensitive-skinned gardeners and Robin warns that you should beware of wearing pale-coloured clothes while handling them, as the plant juices leave permanent brown stains that only appear after clothes have been washed.

### Herbs to try

**Soapwort or 'Bouncing Bet' (*Saponaria officinalis*)** 30-90cm (12-36in), flowering July to September. With soft pink or creamy-white flowers, 'Bouncing Bet' – particularly in the double-flowered form – is an old favourite for cottage garden perennial borders, although the spreading, rhizomatous root system can be invasive and it may be necessary to chop back the underground stems in spring to contain growth. For sun or part-day shade on most soils. Divide in autumn or spring. **Uses** As the name implies, the roots and leaves make an ideal soap substitute. One gardener at Hardwick used soapwort root to remove oil stains from clothing and it has been used by National Trust conservators in textile restoration.

**French Tarragon (*Artemisia dracunculus*)** To 90cm (3ft). French tarragon has long, narrow, dark green leaves spiralling up stiff stems and spreads by underground runners when well-suited. The little green flowers do not usually open or set seed in the cool British climate. Russian tarragon (*Artemisia dracunculus dracunculoides*), a much hardier, more vigorous form, has paler green leaves and often sets seed in Britain. Although the two are often confused, the flavour is greatly inferior to the French. Plant in spring in a warm, sunny position on light, sharply drained soil. Robin finds that French tarragon lives up to its tender reputation. Lift, divide and move to fresh soil every few years in spring. Cut back dead top growth in April. Propagate from semi-ripe cuttings in late summer or by division in spring. **Uses** The name comes from the French 'estragon', meaning 'little dragon', and stems from belief that it could cure the bites and stings of poisonous animals and insects. Use sparingly. Chop into melted butter to accompany mushrooms, asparagus and courgettes as well as the usual salad dressings or garnish for steak and fish.

### Maintenance and planting tips

● **Regular rotation of herbs is essential**, not just for the Lamiaceae family, but for most others too. 'We embarked on regular replanting about fifteen years after the borders were first planted, but it was over-due. Many of our replacement plantings were just petering out. We now rotate herbs as necessary, but in future we will plan a complete redesign every ten to fifteen years.'

● **Feeding herbs** Most herbs are not keen on a rich diet, so do not use any form of fertiliser when planting out. 'For just a few which like more nutrient, like parsley, onions, and other annual herbs, we will add a little pelleted poultry manure at planting. This also helps parsley grow strongly enough to weather the odd attack from carrot root fly.'

● **The amount of wind and frost which your garden receives in winter and spring dictates the time at which you cut back different shrubby herbs.** One of the major maintenance tasks in any herb garden is the point at which you go in and cut back all the top growth which has protected the shrubby plants over the winter – usually early spring. Frost can penetrate the stems of recently pruned shrubs and kill them. We can cut tough *Teucrium chamaedrys* back as early as February, but will sometimes leave the top growth on santolina, hyssop and rue until April. The catch is that you don't want to leave pruning too late, as the plants will waste energy re-growing from the shoot tips before you have pruned. The right time really depends on your own garden conditions.

● **Chop down certain leafy herbs in mid-season, to force them into producing fresh, young foliage.** 'We do this with lovage, comfrey, sweet cicely and angelica, and it also helps to restrain rampant self-sowers.'

● **Winter protection for tender evergreens** Young plants of bay or myrtle can easily be damaged by the weight of heavy snow and Robin also feels that they overwinter better if the 'neck' of the plant is kept as dry as possible. He has invented the Hardwick 'mini-cloche' to protect them. He threads two strands of 3mm wire through a single sheet of 6mm polycarbonate, bends the polycarbonate and twists the base of each wire around strong wooden stilts so that the protective sheet hovers above the plant.

## Seed sowing tips

● Always sow seeds into compost which is moist. 'We overfill the trays with compost, press down to level and firm the surface using a presser board, and then soak the trays from below in warm water until the surface glistens.' Allow to drain for a few minutes before sowing the seeds.

● Cover the seed with roughly twice its own depth of compost, sifted through a 12mm (¹/₈in) sieve.

● After sowing, Robin sets the trays in a heated frame and

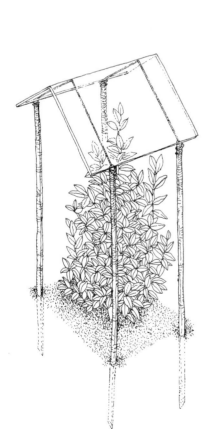

The Hardwick mini-cloche.

a

b

c

Growing herbs from seed. The surface is firmed with a presser board (**a**), and the seed is covered with sieved compost (**b**). Handling the seedlings by their leaves, prick out into individual pots to grow on (**c**).

covers them with a sheet of glass to retain moisture, turning this daily to remove excess condensation. It is rarely necessary to water again until the seeds have germinated, but if the trays dry out, soak them again from below with warm water.

● To hasten germination in parsley, Robin waters the trays again after sowing with very hot water straight from the tap. This helps to settle the seed into the compost and ensures quicker, more even germination. The seeds are not damaged by the heat of the water which starts to cool almost immediately, but is still warm enough to kick-start the parsley.

● At Hardwick, parsley is the only herb for which bottom heat is consistently used, since germination is so temperature dependant. The seedlings are removed from the bottom heat as soon as the seeds have germinated.

## Sowing annual and biennial herbs in cell trays

Although the gardeners at Hardwick have pricked out basil, sweet marjoram, coriander and parsley from standard seed trays in the past, Robin now finds that they produce stronger plants if root disturbance is avoided by sowing directly into cell trays.

● Basil, coriander and sweet marjoram are sown in mid-April and parsley in March. We use cell trays with a root run of approximately 2·5 cm (1 in) square and a little deeper.

● Half fill each tray with a good quality seed compost and sow two or three seeds per station. Robin finds that by sowing as many as four or five seeds per cell for basil, many problems that are caused by over-watering are overcome. 'I think that this method creates so much competition for moisture that the area where the neck of the seedling sits remains drier.'

● The trays are then set in the greenhouse which is kept at a minimum temperature of 10°c (50°F). Again, the trays are covered with glass or polythene.

Direct-sticking semi-ripe cuttings in a cold frame.

● When the young seedlings have plenty of top growth, pot into 9cm (3½in) pots to grow on and make a strong root system. Robin plants out in June after the last danger of frost.

## 'Direct-sticking' semi-ripe cuttings in a cold frame

Huge numbers of short-lived shrubby plants are propagated from semi-ripe cuttings taken in the first week of September, using a very simple technique – just garden soil and an unheated cold frame.

● The cold frames are filled to a depth of 45cm (18in) with ordinary, unsterilised garden soil.

● Semi-ripe cuttings from shrubby herbs such as sage, lavender, santolina, thyme, artemisia, *Helichrysum italicum*, *Teucrium chamaedrys* and others are taken by the usual method (see Bateman's p.22) and then stuck directly into the soil about 2·5cm (1in) apart.

● The cold frames are kept closed to prevent the cuttings wilting before they have rooted and in sunny weather are covered with green mesh shading, again to prevent wilting.

● When cuttings are rooted – usually by the end of October – the frames will be ventilated for an hour or so each day in sunny, frost-free weather. Robin usually achieves a ninety per cent success rate.

● In March, the cuttings are potted up individually, using 9cm (3½in) pots for most. More vigorous shrubs such as sage will be potted into 11cm (4in) pots.

## Robin's favourite herbs

**Lovage (*Levisticum officinale*)** To 3m (6ft) or more, flowering June and July. A tall, striking perennial, with a strong aroma and taste of celery. Lovage has hollow stems like angelica and glossy, bright green leaves divided into broad segments. The large heads of yellow-green flowers are held in the umbrella-like shape typifying its relations. Robin describes it as 'very architectural – but we cut it down in mid-season when the flowerheads are setting seed to allow it to divert energy into producing fresh foliage for cutting from the base. Otherwise it becomes rather tatty.' Growing naturally by streams, a rich, moist soil in sun suits it best, but it is tough enough for almost any garden soil, including heavy clay. Divide in autumn or spring and sow seed in spring. **Uses** A popular medicinal and culinary herb – particularly with the Greeks and Romans – although less commonly used today. Medicinally it has been used to treat flatulence and colic in children as well as to cure jaundice and urinary problems. Today the essence distilled from lovage is used in perfumery and liquor distillation.

**Alecost or Costmary (***Tanacetum balsamita***)** 30-150cm (12-60in), flowering August to October. An aromatic perennial whose finely hairy, toothed and pointed leaves look almost like an annual nettle and have a fresh taste and smell of cucumber and spearmint. Little yellow button flowers. Plant in spring on well-drained soil in a sunny position. Divide the creeping rootstock in spring. **Uses** This was a popular medieval herb whose leaves were added to salads and soups and used for flavouring roast meats. Medicinally it has been used to treat upset stomachs, influenza and dysentery. 'I'm afraid it's the beer angle I like here!' says Robin. 'The common name comes from its use as a spicy flavouring in brewing.'

## Tips for using herbs

● **Gwyn Allan's rosemary biscuits**

50g (2oz) sugar
150g (6oz) wholemeal
   flour

1 tablespoon fresh chopped
   or dried rosemary
100g (4oz) butter

Sift the sugar, flour and rosemary thoroughly together in a mixing bowl. Rub in the butter and then knead to a workable dough. Take the mixture and roll it into small balls. Set these on a greased baking tray and flatten each with a fork. Bake in an oven at 190°C (375°F, Gas Mark 5) for 10-15 minutes.

● **Rose pot pourri** Use rose petals and buds, lavender flowers, a sprig of rosemary and leaves of scented geraniums to make pot pourri. Spread the flowers and leaves on trays in a warm, dark, but reasonably well-ventilated place (an airing cupboard will do) and turn them regularly. When dry, mix them with crushed whole cloves, cinnamon and allspice and bind with proprietary 'pot pourri' maker.

● **To make a cleansing soapwort decoction**, boil pieces of the root in water for four to five minutes, cool and strain. The decoction may be used as a shampoo or skin lotion, as well as for cleaning delicate fabrics.

● **Tarragon vinegar** Fill a glass jar with fresh leaves, cover with good quality wine vinegar and leave to stand for two months. Use in vinaigrettes or to make mayonnaise.

# Springhill

CO. LONDONDERRY

Area: 18 ha (45 acres)
Soil: Heavy clay, alkaline
Altitude: 30 m (100 ft)
Average rainfall: 889 mm (35 in)
Average climate: Cold winters;
    warm and wet summers

The house and garden at Springhill in County Londonderry were created by the Conynghams, seventeenth-century Scottish settlers who came to the mountains, streams and forests of Ulster with the blessing of the English Crown. Within the charming limestone walls, the Conynghams created a graciously formal, intimate garden with a serene white Dovehouse, delightful cobbled drying yard and an abundance of herbaceous planting overflowing in the moist climate.

Locally, Springhill has long been known for its herbs and, although the history and cultivation of these – especially the camomile lawn – is unclear, they may well have first become a feature during the nineteenth century. The story goes that guests were always cajoled into viewing the garden before dinner – and in particular the very unusual feature of the camomile lawn. Coaxed to its brink, they were encouraged by the proud owners to remove boots and experience its scented, sensual pleasures on their tired, dusty feet. The ritual over, dinner was served in the sure knowledge that everyone's evening would be sweetened, courtesy of the lawn.

JOHN BOYLE has been caring for the garden at Springhill since 1997, arriving in 1995 from a previous incarnation in the building trade, just as the original National Trust gardener, Emmett Martin, was about to retire. Watching him at work in the intimate surroundings, you instantly feel that gardening is not just another job for John, but something deeply felt. He absorbs his horticultural lessons directly from the plants for which he cares, minutely observing their reactions to his various ministrations and adjusting his technique to suit. Caring for the camomile lawn is a labour of love, and he finds it hard to count the hours he has spent on hands and knees carefully transferring plants from areas where they luxuriate to sparse patches in need of thickening.

## Herbs at Springhill

The garden 'rooms' at Springhill are modest enough to provide the visitor with inspiration for any typically small, modern garden and the little herb garden is no exception. Branching off a long, formal path lined with the pencil shapes of Irish juniper (*Juniperus communis* 'Hibernica'), it is like a small anteroom, serving as an introduction to the larger living rooms of a house. Each of the three sides is backed by a wall with a different aspect. Lemon balm, parsley, chives, lovage and a variety of mints thrive against the shadier east-facing wall, while rosemary, southernwood, tansy, sage, lavender and thyme enjoy the sunnier south- and west-facing positions. Slates partition the herb borders vertically to prevent the excessive spread of creeping mints and thymes – particularly useful where more than one cultivar is grown.

Usually as you ascend a hill, the soil below your feet becomes progressively drier – Springhill, with its seven underground streams, flies in the face of expectation and the ground becomes wetter the higher you climb. Add to this a damp, cold winter and a heavy clay soil and you have less than ideal conditions for the majority of Mediterranean herbs. The successes at Springhill show what may be achieved with persistent, intelligent cultivation. Raised beds help ensure adequate drainage despite the abundant spring water and the wet climate, and the soil is regularly improved with a top-dressing of organic matter. John observes that year by year, conditions are more to the liking of the herbs he grows.

### The camomile lawn
Camomile is naturally a small, creeping herb of wasteland and field in Mediterranean regions, enjoying a light, sandy soil and sunny climate. Springhill could hardly be a less likely home and yet the small square of green which centres the herb garden has been maintained – and improved – over the years against the odds as it suffers from quite heavy foot traffic. This is also the cause of the second major problem – invasion by annual meadow grass, dandelion and daisy, which are carried in on the feet of visitors. While the grass and weeds thrive in the warm, damp climate, the rain reduces the vigour of the camomile, hampering its ability to spread itself by little runners or 'tillers' to smother out the weeds.

BELOW: The non-flowering variety of camomile *Chamaemelum nobile* 'Treneague' will provide the highest quality lawn.

RIGHT: The camomile lawn at Springhill.

Weed infestation has caused the lawn to be lifted and reset on three separate occasions since the Trust took over the garden in 1959. Fortunately the small area involved – only 6·5 m (21½ ft) long by 2·4 m (8 ft) wide – ensures that the cost involved is not prohibitive. Another rule, perhaps, for the would-be camomile gardener – guard against excessive ambition when you first plan your lawn! Less is definitely more…

At each replant, the soil has been sterilised with dazomet in autumn to kill ungerminated weed seeds, with a cover of polythene laid in position over the winter to retain the fumes. In spring, the polythene is removed and the soil improved with a mixture of 50:50 peat and sharp sand lightly forked in. The lawn takes about three years to fill in by the 'tillering' growth of the camomile until it forms a complete cover.

## Planting and maintaining a camomile lawn

With all this talk of damage to the lawn, John does not want to leave the impression that camomile is in any sense a delicate thing. 'It's a tough plant and puts up with a lot, given a good start in the right conditions.'

● Use the non-flowering variety of lawn camomile called 'Treneague' for the highest quality lawn. The long, sprawling flowering stems of the flowering form will need to be removed with shears for a passably neat lawn effect.

● If you buy lawn camomile from a good herb nursery, you will usually be supplied with small clumps, ready for division (**a**). These you can split immediately on arrival and plant out, or you can pot them up into seed trays, about six divisions to a standard seed tray (**b**). Grow on for four to five months in a cold frame, by which time the camomile will usually have tripled itself and you will be able to divide it again at planting.

● Improve the soil using 50:50 peat or a coir-based soil improver and sharp sand just as John does and rake the surface completely level, removing large clods or stones.

Establishing a camomile lawn. Small clumps of camomile supplied by a nursery may be divided and grown on in seed trays in a cold frame to increase your stock (**a** & **b**). Small divisions taken from areas where the camomile is growing thickly may be transplanted to parts of the lawn where coverage is sparser (**c**).

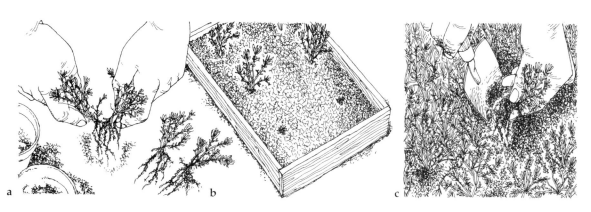

a                                    b                                    c

● Plant the divisions out about 10–15 cm (4–6 in) apart. Water in thoroughly and check for weeds at least once a week during the first season. Once established, the lawn may require watering in conditions of drought.

● Each spring, John top-dresses the lawn with fine grade, sieved peat and sharp sand, laying a layer of about 1·75–5 cm (1½–2 in) over the top and very gently brushing this in.

● It is crucial to keep the lawn growing vigorously so that it smothers self-sown grasses. If your lawn has suffered during the winter, encourage spring growth with a very weak, high nitrogen liquid feed, diluted to one quarter of the manufacturer's recommended strength.

● Use a hover mower in spring, or carefully rake with a springbok. Both encourage the thickening of the lawn by 'tillering'. Walking on it – within reason – has the same effect.

● John regularly inspects the lawn for weeds and lifts away small, rooted portions of camomile where the growth is most dense, for replanting into sparser areas (c). 'The little pieces that I have shifted in one year will usually have spread themselves to cover bare soil by the following season,' he says.

● Once camomile is well-established, it competes vigorously with grass seedlings to smother them out, but dandelions and other weeds are a different matter. Therefore, choose an area of the garden where there is less chance of self-sown seedlings – from weeds or border plants – to establish your lawn.

● 'I find it much easier to weed the lawn when the soil is moist,' John comments. 'This is very delicate work and you don't do so much damage on a damp soil.'

## Herbs to try

**Camomile (*Chamaemelum nobile*, syn. *Anthemis nobilis*)** To 22·5 cm (9 in), flowering from mid-summer to autumn. Mat-forming perennial, whose soft, feathery, light green foliage gives off a sweet, apple-like scent when crushed. Plant in spring or autumn in light, well-drained, but moisture-retentive soil in full sun. The flowering form with double or single creamy flowers may be used to edge paths where it will release its scent when occasionally trodden. German camomile (our British native, 'scented mayweed' or *Matricaria recutita*), an annual or biennial with feathery leaves and small white daisy flowers, requires similar conditions. **Uses** An old medieval 'strewing' herb, camomile used also to be known as the 'Plant's Physician', and gardeners would place it next to plants which were growing poorly to aid their recovery. Medicinally used for insomnia, influenza, and migraine. Handling camomile may cause dermatitis.

Clipping bay to promote a bushier plant.

Rosemary (LEFT) and Lemon Balm (RIGHT).

**Bay, Sweet Laurel (*Laurus nobilis*)** To 20m (66ft). This evergreen shrub or small tree from the Mediterranean, with glossy, wavy-edged, lance-shaped leaves is a good choice for the winter herb garden and is very adaptable to cultivation in both informal and formal shapes. **Uses** The specific name '*nobilis*' or 'noble' indicates the esteem in which bay has been held since the Ancient Greeks, who made wreaths known as 'bacca laurea' from its branches to honour emperors, generals, poets or learned men. Our educational use of the term 'Bachelor' may have its origins in this practice. A symbol of good fortune and protection against evil, bay was also used as a 'strewing herb', and a tea made from the leaves used to aid digestion and treat influenza and bronchitis.

Bay appreciates the warmest, sunniest position in the garden. Avoid planting youngsters in windy positions and give them a protective blanket of bracken, horticultural fleece or even bubble-wrap in bitter winter weather during their first few years. Once established they usually require no protection beyond the original choice of a sheltered site for planting. John advises that young bays should be 'tipped back' regularly from the third year to promote bushy plants. He clips the mature specimens at Springhill as often as twice a year in May and September to promote bushiness and cuts away long unshapely leading shoots. Once the leaders are pruned away, the small sideshoots below grow on strongly to give him a luxurious, full shape. Trim with shears rather than hedge-trimmers to avoid a ragged, unsightly look for the following few months and never prune after September, since the young growth promoted by late pruning is more susceptible to winter damage. See also Gunby Hall, p.30.

## John's favourite herbs

**Variegated Lemon Balm (*Melissa officinalis* 'Variegata')** 30-60cm (12-24in), flowering June to October. With its oval, rather rough, bright leaves of green and gold, this sweetly lemon-scented herb makes useful groundcover even in quite heavy shade on poor soils. The name 'melissa' is derived from the Greek for honeybee, because the clustered white or pinkish flowers attract bees. Best on rich, moisture-retentive soil in sun or shade. Divide in spring or autumn and cut two to three times in summer to promote fresh growth for harvesting. **Uses** Recommended by the Romans 'to make the heart merry', used as a herbal tea for promoting relaxation and sleep. Also used for herb sauces and marinades. John likes its decorative colouring in the garden, but also hangs a few leaves in netting under the running bath tap after a hard day's work, to relieve his aches and pains.

**Rosemary (***Rosmarinus officinalis***)** To 2m (6½ft), flowering April to June. The casual, slightly sprawling habit, bright blue flowers and narrow evergreen leaves which have a wonderful fragrance when crushed make this deservedly one of the most popular shrubby herbs. There are more varieties to choose from than you might think: white-flowered 'Albus'; erect 'Miss Jessopp's Upright'; sprawling Prostratus Group; a slow-growing gold-variegated form, 'Aureus', sometimes called 'gilded' rosemary; compact, cascading, bright blue 'Benenden Blue'; 'Severn Sea' with violet-blue flowers and spreading, arching habit; 'Majorca Pink', a slightly tender, pink-flowered variety; and clear blue, slightly tender 'Sissinghurst Blue'. A characterful plant, rosemary is best left to grow unpruned, perhaps with long leaders in danger of spoiling the overall shape of the shrub cut back no later than July to ensure the regrowth of plenty of new flowering wood before winter. Plant in spring into dry, well-drained, preferably alkaline, soil in full sun. Like all evergreens, it requires a position sheltered from wind. Propagate from semi-ripe cuttings in late summer.
**Uses** Traditionally thought to ward off evil spirits, protect against disease and strengthen the memory – so much so that Greek scholars sitting exams would wear a garland around the head. Also used to flavour sweet dishes like jellies, jams and biscuits. A tea made with the herb is believed to revive invalids and alleviate depression or anxiety. 'When I'm passing I'll pull a bit off and take a sniff of it every now and again,' says John. 'It really helps clear the head.'

## Tips for using herbs

Juniper

● **Camomile tea** Pick flowers for drying just before they are in full bloom, without their stalks, in midsummer. Dry them rapidly in a dark, well-ventilated place at about 35°C (95°F). Make the tea with a cupful of dried flowerheads steeped in boiling water for 15–20 minutes and strained. Mix with honey and lemon and use it for soothing the nerves, aiding digestion and promoting sound sleep.

● **Juniper berry wine** Put 50g (2oz) of crushed berries in 750ml (1½pts) of white wine and macerate for a fortnight, shaking the mixture up once every three to four days. Strain and drink a health-giving wineglass a day. Juniper should be avoided by pregnant women as some forms have abortive properties.

● **Lemon balm tea** Believed to promote a long life! Infuse 25g (1oz) of leaves or flowering tips in 250–500ml (½–1pt) of boiling water for 5 minutes. Try the tea combined with a little peppermint and honey to calm the stomach and induce sleep.

# Buckland Abbey

DEVON

---

Area: 1·2 ha (3 acres)
Soil: Light, shaly loam, acidic
Altitude: 76m (250ft)
Average rainfall: 1016mm
    (40in)
Average climate: Wet and mild
    winters with frost; wet and
    warm summers

---

Originally a Cistercian monastery, Buckland Abbey was purchased in the sixteenth century by Devon's famous Elizabethan seafarer, Sir Francis Drake, and remained in the hands of his family into the twentieth century. There is now little trace of the formal, possibly Tudor, garden shown in an engraving by Samuel and Nathaniel Buck, dated 1734. In spite of the sweeping twentieth-century lawns fringed with mature trees and flowering shrubs, it is the original Cistercian custodianship – with the cider orchard, beehives, vegetables and herbs – which echoes here most strongly. Although the Herb Garden is modern in design, it is richly stocked with plants that would have been familiar friends and daily allies for the brothers at Buckland Abbey.

---

SALLY WHITFIELD has been the sole full-time gardener at Buckland Abbey since 1988 and not only cares for the grounds within the immediate environs of the Abbey, but is also out in all weathers to help with general estate maintenance, including woodland work. During her earlier career, she worked as a volunteer, helping to maintain the many coastal paths for which the Trust is responsible in South Devon. 'Originally the job was described as 'mostly lawn or path maintenance and keeping borders tidy', but it has expanded with the years. I am now head of both the garden and the estate, involved in helping to organise some of the regular social events. In January, for example, we have the Wassail when we toast the apple trees to encourage them to carry a good crop, singing to them and beating them with sticks. There's Morris dancing, cider cake and punch and then we finish by firing guns through their branches. I think the monks would be pleased to see the chickens and the thriving orchard, but what they'd say to the Morris dancing, I dread to think!'

## Herbs at Buckland Abbey

The Herb Garden was probably laid out after a visit by Vita Sackville-West to Buckland Abbey in 1953, in her capacity as a member of the Trust's Garden Committee. She is believed to have advised that the small, sunny, south-west facing triangle between the Abbey and the Great Barn would make an ideal herb garden, in keeping with the traditions of the place.

The design shows what may be done with dwarf hedges on the kind of undulating, slightly irregular site which seems to militate against formality. The intimate arrangement offers fifty-four precise little compartments for cultivating different herbs. Sally has added an ingenious touch of her own to enhance the overall 'knot garden' effect. Almost imperceptibly she varies the height to which she shears the hedging, trimming for the tallest hedging on the high ground and gradually tapering the height away as the ground dips.

## Herb garden patterns worked in box

Dwarf box (*Buxus sempervirens* 'Suffruticosa') is a good choice for creating a hedge-patterned garden, since it is much longer-lived than any of the older traditional 'hedging' herbs such as lavender, wall germander and thyme. While the Herb Garden at Buckland could not strictly be classified as a 'knot garden', it demonstrates the adaptability of the traditional style. The box hedges planted in the 1950s have never been replaced although severe pruning was required to rejuvenate and restore their formality during the 1980s.

● The patterns of the box hedging at Buckland allow a variety of different plant habits and heights to be rationalised within a strong framework.

● Sally grows a different herb within each compartment which allows her to plan localised soil treatments to suit each plant. Parsley and chives, for instance, like a richer diet than most herbs so may have the soil manured before planting.

● The compartments make for easier rotation of those herbs which suffer from soil-borne diseases such as mint rust or the 'soil sickness' of members of the sage and lavender family.

● Box competes with the herbs for nutrients, ensuring that the soil is not too rich for herbs that like a lean diet. Sally advises, 'You are best just to get the herbs in and let them get on with it, without feeding. When I have fed or manured some portions of the garden, the herbs often respond by growing in a patchy way and may refuse to cover the ground.'

● The box hedging supplies the slightly more tender herbs such as hyssop and French or Spanish lavender (*Lavandula stoechas*) with a little protection during winter.

● On the debit side, Sally finds that the box is the ideal hiding place for snails. 'You can plant a soft-leaved herb such as hyssop out one day and come out the following morning to find it's vanished! I sink plastic drinking beakers full of beer up to their rims just inside the hedge as traps.'

● Overhanging herbs with large leaves such as elecampane and comfrey can be very hard on the box and leave bald patches on its foliage.

● Maintenance of the box hedges is quite labour-intensive, since they must be clipped once or twice a year.

LEFT: The Herb Garden at Buckland Abbey. The 'knot garden' design of the box hedging provides a strong framework which allows different herbs to be cultivated in individual compartments.

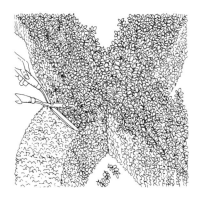

Trimming box hedging. At Buckland Abbey the gardeners clip the sides back first to enable them to get the angles along the top accurate.

## Establishing and maintaining box hedging

● Plan the design on paper first and keep the pattern simple: a high standard of maintenance – which takes time – is essential to the beauty of the design.

● Before planting, ensure that the site is raked perfectly level and transfer your design to the ground using bamboo canes, string and sand to mark out the lines of the hedging. Check and double check – preferably from above – for lines which are not perfectly true.

● Lightly fork a slow-release, balanced fertiliser into the soil before planting.

● Young dwarf box plants about 15cm (6in) high should be set out at approximately 15-22.5cm (6-9in) spacings along the lines of the pattern. Sally will plant out youngsters in the third spring after the season when she took cuttings.

● Start clipping the hedge from the second summer after planting and clip at least once a year. The Buckland hedges are trimmed between the end of July and August. Don't clip any later than this, so that the young growth which clipping promotes has a chance to 'harden off' before the first frosts.

● Sally uses shears and tackles the sides first. She then clips the tops all at the same time, which allows her to get the angles she wants on the top of the hedge consistently true.

● Old box hedges which have become unshapely will take rough treatment to rejuvenate them, cutting right back into the old wood. If you are nervous about being too extreme, try cutting back one side and the top of the hedge in the first season, completing the other side in the second year. Feed the hedge to encourage growth after cutting back.

● Sally strongly recommends an annual feed for box hedges in any herb garden, because the herbs deprive box of a good deal of the nutrients which are important for vigorous growth.

## Propagating box from semi-ripe cuttings

Fortunately, since box is such an important feature at Buckland, box cuttings may be successfully rooted with a minimum of fuss in a spare corner of the vegetable plot. Sally finds she will have a good, young box hedge growing on in its final position in as little as four years after taking her cuttings.

● Sally uses the clippings from her August trimming of the hedges as cuttings – these are usually about 7.5-10cm (3-4in) in length. None of the basal leaves is removed from the cuttings, and they are simply left with the single cut where they were sheared from the hedge.

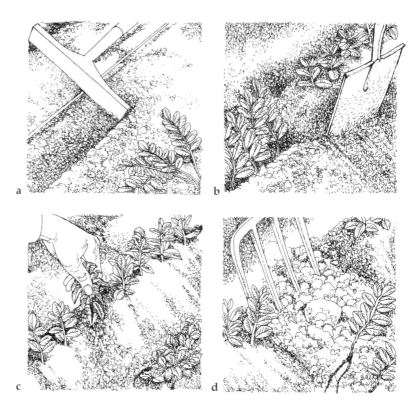

Propagating box from
semi-ripe cuttings.

● 'I find that the best cuttings come from the tops of the hedges – the growth is more vigorous and upright.

● She takes out a trench about 20cm (4in) deep and lines the base with a 5cm (2in) layer of silver sand (**a**).

● The clippings are set into the ground in handfuls (**b**). 'You don't have to be too fussy about this – just push them in in clumps and draw the soil up over the base. They root better when they are really packed in. If you set them in individually, I find they are all inclined to rot off,' she advises.

● About 9 or 12 months on, in the following summer, the cuttings should be well-rooted and Sally finds she gets at least a sixty per cent success rate. Cuttings which have failed to root and turned brown are removed; the rest remain until the following spring (**c**). Each cutting will by now have produced one long root rather than a mass of fibrous roots.

● In the second spring after the cuttings were taken, they are finally lifted with a spade or garden fork and lined out in position, spacing them about 15–22.5cm (6-9in) apart (**d**). Don't worry about breaking the long root slightly when you lift them, since this will encourage a more fibrous root system.

● Before planting, Sally forks a balanced fertiliser into the soil to encourage the young plants to establish new root systems.

Box

Hyssop

Lemon Thyme

# Herbs to try

**Box (*Buxus sempervirens*)** 2-5m (6-15ft). With small, neat, rounded leaves and dense, compact growth which responds beautifully to clipping, box is a tree or shrub which has been used since Classical times in garden topiary. The common name comes from the use of its wood in box manufacture. A pretty, slower growing, silver-variegated cultivar called 'Elegantissima' is worth trying, but it is *B. sempervirens* 'Suffruticosa' (to 75cm/30in) which is the most common 'edging' box. **Uses** A narcotic herb, once used to treat malaria, although rarely today due to its toxicity. Now used in homeopathy to treat rheumatism.

**Hyssop (*Hyssopus officinalis*)** 45-60cm (18-24in). With tiny, aromatic, lance-shaped leaves and soft spikes of blue, pink or white flowers in late summer, hyssop is a semi-evergreen perennial with a woody base, very attractive to butterflies and bees. Since it responds well to hard pruning in spring, it makes a good edging or low, informal hedging herb. Plant in spring in a sunny, well-drained to dry soil. Leave top growth on over winter to protect the woody base from frost and clip back to old wood in late March/April. Propagate from seed in spring or by softwood cuttings in summer. **Uses** The name comes from the Greek for 'a holy herb' and refers to its use in cleansing holy places. Hyssop teas and baths are old remedies for rheumatism, coughs and sore throats. Excessive use may be dangerous and it should never be taken by pregnant women.

**Thyme** Many of the 350 different species attract bees and make neat, small-leaved, ground-covering subjects with a powerful aroma for use as edging or 'infill' plants in the herb garden. Some species are very prostrate and creeping (for example *T. praecox*, *T. serpyllum*) while others are more erect (*T. mastichina*) or hummock-forming (forms of *T. vulgaris*, *T. pulegioides*). All are drought-tolerant and the most prostrate forms do well if planted between in paved areas, to sprawl over and soften the hard lines. Plant in spring on very light, sharply drained soil in full sun. Take softwood cuttings in summer or semi-ripe cuttings in late summer. (See Gunby Hall, p.28, for Irishman's cuttings.) **Uses** From the ancient civilisations, thyme has been closely associated with death and the souls of the dead were thought to live among its flowers. The Egyptians used it in their embalming ointments and it was also used in the medieval and Elizabethan posies or 'tussie mussies', which were carried to ward away smells and contagion.

**Lemon Thyme (*T.* × *citriodorus*)** To 30cm (12in) high, spreading to 60cm (24in). Pale lilac-pink flowers. A variable, hummock-forming to prostrate shrublet, hybrid between

*T. pulegioides* and *T. vulgaris*, with strong, lemon scent. Most common use is in cookery or aromatherapy. Good variegated cultivars such as 'Bertram Anderson' (gold and green) and 'Silver Queen' (silver and green) are extremely ornamental, although 'Silver Queen' is amongst the least hardy thymes and also has a tendency to revert to plain green leaves.

**Caraway Thyme (*T. herba-barona*)** To 10cm (4in) high, spreading to 60cm (24in). Wiry-stemmed little shrublet with tiny, dark green leaves and a prostrate habit. Pink or pale purple flowers. Has strong caraway, nutmeg or lemon scent, varying from plant to plant. Associated with flavouring for a 'baron' of roast beef. Also in meat dishes where garlic is used.

**Spanish Wood Marjoram, Mastic Thyme (*T. mastichina*)** To 30cm (12in) high, spreading to 75cm (30in). White flowers. Erect, small shrublet, with downy leaves smelling of camphor or eucalyptus, sometimes used to flavour meat dishes. Commercially, the oil is known as 'oil of wild marjoram' and is used to flavour meat sauces and soups.

**Creeping or Wild Thyme (*T. praecox*)** To 5cm (2in) high, spreading to 45cm (18in). Mauve or purple flowers. Very prostrate and mat-forming. May be used in cooking.

**Broad or Large-leaved Thyme (*T. pulegioides*)** To 25cm (10in) high, spreading to 45cm (18in). Pink, purple flowers. Small, sprawling shrublet. Can replace *T. vulgaris* in cooking.

**Wild, Creeping or 'Mother of Thyme' (*T. serpyllum*)** To 7cm (3in) high, spreading to 1m (3ft). Pink, purple or red flowers. Very prostrate shrubby herb, with creeping stems. Used in cooking, like *T. vulgaris*. Try also *T. serpyllum* var. *albus* (white flowers), *T. serpyllum coccineus* (red flowers), 'Annie Hall' (pale pink flowers), 'Minor' (slow-growing and compact), and 'Russetings' (dark bronze foliage and pink flowers).

**Common Thyme, Garden Thyme (*T. vulgaris*)** To 45cm (18in) high, spreading to 45cm (18in). White to pale purple flowers. Small, variable, shrublet. An essential ingredient in *bouquet garni* and French cuisine, especially slow-cooking dishes since it retains the flavour well. It can also help to control flea beetle and cabbage white butterfly in companion plantings. 'Silver Posie' is perhaps the prettiest of the silver-variegated thymes, although quite prone to loss during the winter at Buckland, while 'Erectus' is very upright in habit.

## Sally's favourite herbs

**Mullein, Aaron's Rod (*Verbascum thapsus*)** To 2m (6ft), flowering mid-summer. Biennial with lovely, grey-green basal rosettes of foliage and tall, architectural spikes of yellow flower. Plant in spring in a sunny position on well-drained

*Thymus serpyllum*

Mullein

Elecampane

Lemon Verbena

soil – especially successful on dry, stony soils or in a gravel garden. **Uses** According to Homer, this was the plant that Ulysses took to protect himself from Circe and it has long been attributed with the power of driving away evil spirits. Medicinally used for chest complaints.

**Elecampane, Scabwort (*Inula helenium*)** To 1·5m (5ft). A tall, structurally strong, stout-stemmed plant with cheerful yellow daisies like little sunflowers from mid-summer to autumn, elecampane can make a good central 'peak' or focal point for a large, decorative herb border. Produces a camphor-scented essential oil. Plant in spring or autumn in moist, well-drained soil in full sun. Divide in spring or autumn. **Uses** The species name for elecampane may derive from a legendary association with Helen of Troy, from whose tears it was claimed to have grown after she had been seized by Paris. Contains inulin, which is sometimes recommended to diabetics as a food sweetener. The roots used to be candied and eaten as a sweetmeat or sucked as lozenges to ease whooping cough and sore throats. Internally the roots have been used to treat bronchitis and hay fever, but are never given to pregnant women.

**Lemon Verbena (*Aloysia triphylla*, syn. *Lippia citriodora*)** Deciduous shrub to 3m (10ft), but much smaller in the British climate where – if it survives the winter – it will die back and reshoot in spring. Small white flowers in summer. Only tolerant of temperatures down to about –5°c (23°F), lemon verbena may be risked in the open garden at the base of a warm, sunny south- or west-facing wall, provided that cuttings are taken annually as an insurance policy. May be grown in pots in a frost-free greenhouse or porch during winter. Guard against over-watering during winter dormancy. **Uses** A powerful scent for pot pourri and also used as a mildly sedative tea to treat feverish colds and indigestion.

## Tips for using herbs

● **Deterring house flies and blow flies** Sprigs of horehound are laid on the windowsills of the restaurant at Buckland to help keep flies at bay. You can also float a few sprigs in milk to keep those wretched blow flies off.

● **Flowers for salads** The Buckland cooks like to colour up green salads with the flowers of herbs – nasturtiums are particularly popular. Try it yourself, as well as pot marigold, heart's ease (viola) and borage. Remove the bristly green outer sepals from borage first. Use individual petals, entire small flowers or chop the flowers up and sprinkle them over the top just before you serve the salad. Young, succulent nasturtium leaves may also be chopped and used to give a spicy flavour.

# Beningbrough Hall

YORKSHIRE

Area: 3·65 ha (9 acres)
Soil: Silty clay loam, neutral
Altitude: 15 m (50 ft)
Average rainfall: 762 mm (30 in)
Average climate: Cold, wet
  winters; warm, moist
  summers

The garden at Beningbrough Hall was first laid out in the early eighteenth century. The old Walled Garden must, from its earliest days, have been the productive centre, providing a sheltered microclimate which is noticeably warmer and un-ruffled by wind even in the depths of winter. Subsequent planting was bound to flow out from the protective backbone of the combined Hall and garden walls. Lavender hedging now billows at the warm brick base of the Hall and, tucked to right and left in the embrace of yew hedges, are the pleasing patterns of the east and west formal gardens, planted in the Edwardian style with roses, low silver-leaved shrubs, fine foliage perennials, and annuals in blazing colours.

JOHN THALLON trained as a landscape historian and gardened at Beningbrough Hall for fifteen years before he became Head Gardener in 1992, leading the staff of three. He was fascinated to research the Victorian and Edwardian heyday of the Walled Garden, even before restoration began in 1995, discovering that it functioned as a perfect, small-scale economic unit with prodigious output. 'Thomas Foster was Head Gardener here for thirty-eight years until his death in 1866 and he is still remembered in the horticultural world for his introduction of two fine vine cultivars, 'Foster's Seedling' and 'Lady Downes Seedling', both of his own raising. In his day there were seven glasshouses on the site, where now we have one, and the enclosing walls were heated by furnaces and flues within the wall cavity. I've been told that the fires were last lit in the autumn of 1939 and during the war the lawns at Beningbrough were ploughed up for planting pota-toes, as in many large gardens of this size. Hopefully Thomas would be cheered by our restoration work. It used to be so sad to walk through these gates into a derelict field, if you stopped to consider that it should have been Beningbrough's 'heart'. Now I walk in and feel that the heart is beating again.'

## Herbs at Beningbrough Hall

One of the difficulties encountered by the Trust since garden restoration work began during the 1970s has been lack of information about the horticultural life of the grounds over the centuries. As a private estate with a productive kitchen garden, herbs would mainly have been grown for culinary use. A small, practical, herb border set out in rows and regu-larly used by the restaurant staff is therefore an integral element in the restoration of the old kitchen garden, as are cold frames for winter and spring crops of lettuce and turnips or old clay forcing pots for tender young shoots of seakale.

Lack of historical detail proved as much a blessing as it was a problem however, since it left the field open for a little modern innovation. 'When faced with this large area which could not be entirely restored to labour-intensive vegetable crops due to limited manpower, we had to decide what else could be done with it which would dovetail with the garden's historic past – and we felt we needed a theme for new plantings,' John comments. 'Perennial herbs – especially decorative varieties – are a fairly obvious choice, since they are 'useful' plants, but are lower in maintenance requirements'.

The Pear Arch – a decorative walkway, sculptured from trained branches of the fruit and lying right at the centre of the garden – has provided the opportunity for herbaceous under-plantings, over a third of which are ornamental herb cultivars. More important, perhaps, are the massive new plantings of lavender – eight thousand plants of eleven different varieties which conveniently flower during July and August when Beningbrough welcomes the majority of its visitors.

### Tips for happy herbs

● **Shelter** Photographs of the garden in 1900 show hedges running like buttresses from the walls out into the huge open centre of the garden, dividing it up still further into smaller, sheltered sections. Subdividing the area with living wind-breaks or artificial semi-permeable screens helps to filter and reduce the strength of the wind in the area. Trellising screens could perhaps be used to provide small, protected areas and a variety of microclimates in smaller gardens.

● **Winter protection for young evergreens** Shrubby evergreen herbs like bay and myrtle are prone to frost and cold damage. Outside the Walled Garden there are large bay trees which top the wall after twenty years of growth. 'Some people would say this was impossible in Yorkshire – I say it's only *just* possible!' laughs John. 'To establish them we wrapped the young plants up with straw palliasses each winter until they were about 1·2m (4ft) high. The palliasses were made by wrapping polythene sheeting around each bay, stapling it together and then stuffing straw down inside for insulation. I didn't have to trim the trees to encourage bushiness – the die-back caused by the cold winter did that for me. We just removed any scorched or dead growth in late March.'

● **Drainage** John finds that regular cultivation and the annual addition of organic matter has definitely helped improve the drainage properties of the silty soil and, if he is determined to experiment with plants requiring very sharp drainage, he

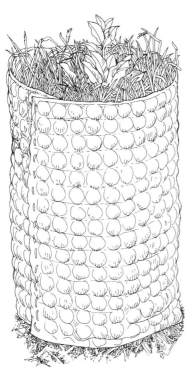

Wrapping evergreens in bubble wrap (or polythene sheeting) for winter protection.

The decorative Pear Arch in the centre of the Kitchen Garden at
Beningbrough, edged with borders of aromatic ornamental herbs.

incorporates pea shingle into the soil at planting. Purple sage (*Salvia officinalis* 'Purpurascens') is the most likely herb to be given this treatment, since John finds it weaker growing than the standard grey-leaved species. If you think your garden has drainage problems try digging 'test holes' of about 1m (3ft) depth in various corners. If you find that water persistently sits in the base during the winter, then it may be worth installing a simple drainage system.

● **Aphid control** John has reinstated the traditional low box hedging shown in the Walled Garden photographs. 'I think there's more to this practice than meets the eye. A survey carried out by the University of Leeds to assess the over-wintering habits of ladybirds discovered that box and euphorbia – and particularly the young, folded leaves at each shoot tip – were extremely popular places for ladybirds to spend the winter. Since they are amongst the most voracious aphid predators, it could well be that the old gardeners new exactly what they were doing when they surrounded the vegetable plots in an old kitchen gardens with a box hedge.'

## Planting and maintaining a lavender hedge

● John advises buying small plants of a given lavender culti-var from a specialist nursery when planting a hedge. Plants grown from your own cuttings are also an acceptable choice for hedging and could be ready to plant out in as little as six or seven months from rooting in late summer (see Barrington Court p.82). John suggests, however, that it would be worth purchasing young stock plants from which to take cuttings. Although cuttings taken from his twenty-year-old hedge at Beningbrough do root, success rates are much lower com-pared with material from young stock plants.

● Other than basic cultivation and levelling, soil for lavender should not require any preparation. John rotavated the turf into the ground in the first season and grew maincrop pota-toes to improve further the soil structure with their fibrous, wide-reaching root systems. He feels that lavender does less well if planted into soil which is overly rich in organic matter.

● For a very broad hedge which gives a good effect even from the second year, try planting lavender in a double, staggered row. John recommends that the two rows of plants should be set about 45cm (18in) apart, with individual plants spaced 45cm (18in) apart in the rows. For a narrower, single row hedge, set the plants at 22·5cm (9in) intervals.

● Always ensure a completely true line for the hedge by set-ting plants out against a garden line, just as when planting vegetables in a row.

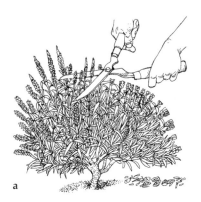
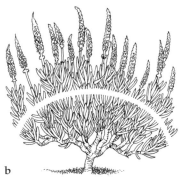

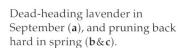

Dead-heading lavender in September (**a**), and pruning back hard in spring (**b**&**c**).

● John retains the visual impact of the plants in flower by planting each cultivar in double rows and harvesting the rows in alternate years – a good trick if you want your plants to do double duty as both flowering and productive plants.

● There are two stages to maintaining an ornamental lavender hedge. In late September, when the bees have finished working the flowers, John deadheads any hedge which has not been harvested for its flowers to prevent self-sown seedlings, clipping it lightly over with shears.

● In late March the following year he clips it again, this time much harder back. 'I trim it to the absolute limit so that there is only a base of leaves left on each plant. You have to use your common sense and experience here. With a cultivar such as 'Imperial Gem' I can remove virtually all the top growth, but a less vigorous cultivar might not put up with this. Certainly an older plant which has not been pruned will not take this kind of treatment. By pruning very hard like this, I can keep plants at exactly the same size for up to ten or fifteen years. But you must do this every year from the time the hedge has achieved the size you want. If you miss a year, that's it, you will never be able to return the hedge to the original size, since you would have to cut back into older, woodier growth and the plants simply will not take it.'

● John starts trimming new hedges from the first spring after planting to encourage the side shoots which make it bushy and thick. Regularly trimmed lavender produces a mass of vigorous new growth each season and has a longer life-span than plants which are simply left to grow in naturally.

● A lavender hedge should never require feeding.

### Herbs to try

**Lavender (*Lavandula* spp.)** With grey, evergreen foliage and soft, pastel-coloured spikes of scented flowers in late summer, lavender is one of the most popular herbs and readily adapts to cultivation as a low hedging plant. Plant in spring on well-drained to dry soil – preferably alkaline – in a sunny position sheltered from cold winter wind. Propagate from semi-ripe cuttings in late summer or from seed, although seedlings tend to be variable in colour of flower and habit. There are about twenty-one different species of lavender native to hot, dry regions around the Mediterranean, the Middle East and India, but only a few Mediterranean species are of real importance, commercially or horticulturally. **Uses** The word 'lavender' is believed to derive from the Latin 'lavare', meaning 'to wash', since the Romans were thought to have added lavender to their bath water for its fragrance and therapeutic properties. Due to its antiseptic and disinfectant properties it was also used as a 'strewing' herb in the Middle Ages. The dried flowers of all lavenders may be used in pot pourri or similar scented preparations, but only L. *angustifolia* is grown for medicinal use of the essential oil. Used internally for depression, tension and migraine headaches, and externally for muscular stiffness, burns and bites.

**Common or English Lavender (L. *angustifolia*, syn. L. *spica*, L. *vera*, L. *officinalis*)** To 60cm (24in). Characterised by narrow, downy, grey-green leaves and long spikes of mauve to purple flowers. The essential oil used in aromatherapy and perfumery comes from the flowers of English lavender.

**'Spike Lavender' (L. *latifolia*)** Virtually never seen in gardens, but grown commercially in Spain for a more pungent oil which is used in cleaning products or as an insect repellant.

**French or Spanish Lavender (L. *stoechas*)** To 90cm (36in). Slightly more tender than English lavender and characterised by the tight clusters – rather than long spikes – of purple flowers held at the tip of each flower-stalk and topped with purple bracts. A decorative plant which will usually survive temperatures of at least $-5°C$ ($23°F$).

**Woolly Lavender (L. *lanata*)** To 60cm (24in). Unfortunately only half-hardy, and not usually able to survive temperatures below $0°C$ ($32°F$), this is a very ornamental lavender with beautiful white, felted leaves. Worth trying at the base of a warm, south- or west-facing wall or as a cool conservatory shrub.

## Choice of lavender cultivars for hedging or flowers

The largest group of cultivated lavenders is composed of hybrids or cultivars (most frequently of L. *angustifolia* and L. *latifolia*) which have been selected for their habit, flower colour and foliage tints. John tends to avoid the white or pink cultivars at Beningbrough Hall, feeling that the strong, deep blues and purples give a better show when planted *en masse*.

In the past he has tried a variety of pink and white-flowered plants and found 'Hidcote White' attractive. He says, however, 'When someone breeds a good, strong, pink-flowered lavender I shall definitely be growing it, but to date I've not really been satisfied with those I have tried.'

**'Hidcote'** 30-60cm (12-24in). Erect and compact, with deep violet flowers held in dense spikes.

**'Munstead'** 30-45cm (12-18in). Good for low hedges with compact growth and early, bright lavender-blue flowers.

**'Grappenhall'** 1-1.2m (3-4ft). Best planted as a single specimen for its late flowers of lavender-blue. Has quite broad leaves and very long flowering stems.

**'Imperial Gem'** To 60cm (24in). With deep purple, short-stemmed flowers and a powerful fragrance, it is said also to resist lavender scab.

**'Folgate'** To 50cm (20in). Compact, violet-flowered cultivar with a strong scent.

**'Ashdown Forest'** To 50cm (20in). Similar to 'Folgate', this is an early cultivar with short flower stems and mid-violet flowers. 'I find this the earliest to flower here – I can sometimes be cutting the flowers in late June,' John comments.

**'Grey Hedge'** 45-53cm (18-21in). Dark purple flower and very good broad, silver leaves, ideal for a hedge.

**'Twickel Purple'** 50-60cm (20-24in). Has a loose growing habit and leaves which sometimes flush purple in winter. Very good, dark purple flower on short stems.

**'Sawyers'** 45-68cm (18-27in). Good grey leaves and large, lavender-blue flowers.

**'Seal'** To 1.5m (5ft). Green foliage and pale mauve flowers.

**'Grosso'** 1.2m (4ft). Wide, spreading habit and long spikes of dark purple flowers. 'This is the weakest cultivar on the Beningbrough soil,' comments John. 'Although it is reputedly one of the best commercial cultivars, it has a long stem which would seem to make harvesting more difficult.'

## John's favourite herbs

**Sweet Cicely (*Myrrhis odorata*)** To 1m (40in), flowering May and June. Highly aromatic herbaceous perennial with divided, softly downy, fern-like leaves and white lace-cap flowers in early summer. Has a very long season of foliage interest, since the lacy foliage appears as early as February and continues to look pretty until it dies back in November. Plant in autumn or spring, ideally in moist, but well-drained soil, in dappled shade, although this is a very tolerant plant, growing

The lavender collection at Beningbrough Hall.

well in most conditions. Propagate by seed sown in spring or by division in autumn and spring. **Uses** The seeds and foliage have both been used as food flavourings for their strongly aniseed taste, in particular the leaves which may be added to *bouquet garni* or used to flavour soups, stews and salads. Recommended as a gentle medicinal herb for digestive upsets. 'This is the only herb which I personally use in cooking, since I am diabetic and it is ideal for sweetening tart apple or rhubarb dishes,' John says. Remove the flowering stems as they emerge to help retain the good flavour of the foliage.

**Variegated Horse-radish (*Armoracia rusticana* 'Variegata')** To 60 cm (2 ft). Horse-radish is a large-leaved plant resembling a dock. Grows even in dense shade, but requires moisture-retentive soil, deeply dug, to which plenty of organic matter has been added. Propagate by root cuttings in late winter, but when plants are lifted even small pieces of root are likely to remain in situ and form new plants. **Uses** Roots used for making horse-radish sauce or peeled and used raw in salads. John uses this lovely form with leaves blotched irregularly in cream for flower arranging.

## Tips for using herbs

● **Sweet cicely with apples** Peel 600g (1½lb) of cooking apples, cut out the cores and cut into slices. Put them in a pan with water to cover the bottom. Tear up two fronds of sweet cicely and add them to take away the tartness of the fruit, remembering to remove these before serving. Cover and cook slowly until the apples are soft, then serve with cream. May also be puréed to make apple sauce.

● **Lavender as an insecticide** Protect drawers and cupboards from moths by rubbing the wood with bunches of foliage, but if you put lavender flowers into a drawer, put them in a muslin bag, sachet, or tie them in an old-fashioned lavender bundle, as the oil is liable to burn small holes in fabric.

● **Lavender bundles** The traditional way to packet fragrant lavender flowers so that they do not come into contact with clothing. Take ten long-stemmed flowers, fix the heads together and bind the stems securely just below the flowerheads with ribbon or thread. Bend back the stems over the flowers, taking care not to crush them, and tie tightly at the top.

# Castle Drogo

DEVON

Area: 5 ha (12 acres)

Soil: Variable, from sandy to clay loam, over rock/shingle; slightly acid to neutral

Altitude: 304 m (1,000 ft)

Average rainfall: 1,143 mm (45 in)

Average climate: Cold, wet winters; warm, damp summers

The threatening walls of Castle Drogo, which rise from a peak overlooking the wilderness of Dartmoor, were built by Edwin Lutyens for wealthy businessman, Julius Drewe, between 1911 and 1931. However, although the astonishing garden, laid out on the rising ground to the north-west of the castle, boldly echoes the architectural style of the building with its massive forbidding wall of immaculately maintained yew, the nuance of its design probably owes less to Lutyens than to the landscape gardener, George Dillistone.

The sheer scale of the garden, with its three terraces and cornerstone arches of the Persian Ironwood tree, *Parrotia persica*, will silence any visitor who stands at its lowest point and gazes upwards towards the oriental tracery of wisteria dripping from the walls of the second terrace. To either side, Lutyens' genius created the bold lines of the twin serpentine paths which wander with deceptive simplicity and absolute regularity through double herbaceous borders.

SARAH BALDWIN first began to garden while working at Bicton College of Agriculture in Devon, before training as a professional gardener at the nearby National Trust garden of Killerton. She spent six years as Head Gardener at Castle Drogo and recently left to take over management of a private German garden. When I spoke to her about the Castle Drogo herbs, just before her departure in the spring of 1998, she was keenly anticipating her new challenge in a continental climate but agreed that she would greatly miss the very special, if not always kind, gardening environment at Castle Drogo. Both she and the second gardener, Eric Robinson, emphasise that wellies are the most usual footwear for a garden perched over Dartmoor. Neither will she forget the hedges... 'They dominate our lives here, just like they dominate the visitors' impression of the garden! We'll spend as many as four days a week from mid-July right through until October clipping them.'

## Herbs at Castle Drogo

When Julius Drewe's grandson, Anthony, bequeathed the garden to the Trust in 1974, the original herb borders on the second level terrace had been planted with azaleas, but in 1989 it was decided to reinstate the herbs. The design by the Trust Garden's Advisor, Paul Miles, has evolved through a variety of stages, but its components serve as strictly ornamental elements in the garden.

The central block plantings of *Santolina pinnata* subsp. *neapolitana*, *Lavandula* 'Munstead' and *Rosmarinus officinalis* flanking the pathway are very strongly structured and sculptural in style with a blocky shape which echoes the fine yew 'walls' surrounding the garden and with softer grey and green foliage to complement the deep rich green of the yew. Behind these are twin colour-themed herb borders which make the most of foliage and flower colours. Each border is centred with scented, winter-flowering *Viburnum farreri*, to provide height. Sarah says, 'They are really flower borders which just happen to use herbs.' The flowering effect of plants in the Apiceae (carrot) family, such as lovage, sweet cicely and fennel is particularly striking as they rise like tall umbrellas, with white or light green flowerheads whose intricate pattern is picked out by the backdrop of the dark yew hedge.

### Herbs to try

The challenge is to find herbs which fit both your design ideas and the climate. Sarah is continually on the watch for golden foliage and flowers, white flowers and scented plants which fulfill the design brief of the original garden plans, but will survive the conditions that posed problems to the health of a few of the border inhabitants.

**Dyer's Camomile**, **Golden Marguerite (*Anthemis tinctoria*)** 20–60cm (8–24in). Biennial or perennial, clump-forming herb with woolly stems and ferny, divided leaves, woolly below. Has creamy-yellow to bright yellow daisy flowers from July to October, attractive to many insects. Certain cultivars are frequently found in ornamental herbaceous borders, such as lemon yellow 'E. C. Buxton' and 'Sauce Hollandaise' with pale cream, almost white flowers. Sunny position on well-drained soil. Clip back in spring, since the top growth offers winter protection. Propagate by spring division or basal cuttings. **Uses** The flowers are used to dye cloth yellow.

**Wall Germander (*Teucrium chamaedrys*)** To 30cm (12in). An aromatic little evergreen sub-shrub with creeping root system. Fairly stiff, upright, hairy stems are clad in small, neat, shiny green leaves, producing little clusters of unspectacular pink flowers along the length of the stem from June to early autumn. Full sun on almost any soil. Grows well in dry-stone walls. Leave top growth on over winter to protect plants. Propagate by cuttings in autumn and spring or by division in spring. **Uses** A medicinal herb which has been used in the past as a tea to cure gout and was said to be effective in allaying asthmatic coughs. Due to its effects as a stimulant and tonic, it is most frequently used now in alcoholic drinks.

Dyer's camomile

*Santolina pinnata* subsp. *neapolitana*

## Choice and maintenance of hedging herbs for garden patterns

'The strong simple patterns and blocks work in the design context of the larger garden,' Sarah says. 'The plant chosen obviously has to be a low, bushy evergreen but, it must be able to take regular hacking back. You can do this to many obliging herbs for a limited period of time, but eventually you must replace them since older shrubby herbs sometimes become less attractive. It is useful to have cuttings coming along – or a good herb nursery nearby!' Sarah gives the plants used at Castle Drogo a life of between five and eight years, except perhaps for longer-lived rosemary which is never clipped.

As well as cotton lavender and lavender, coloured sages, wall germander and curry plant (*Helichrysum italicum*) could be used. Generally these hedging herbs should be planted at a distance of 22·5–45 cm (9–18 in) apart, depending on the plant chosen, but close spacings rarely present problems and techniques such as planting in staggered rows can help to fill in a pattern quite rapidly so that individual plants are not noticeable after the first season. Most herbs used in this way are best clipped once yearly in spring after the worst danger of frost is over or later in summer after flowering.

**Cotton Lavender (*Santolina* spp.)** The three common types of cotton lavender are all used in the schemes at Castle Drogo. *S. chamaecyparissus* (to 60 cm/24 in if allowed to flower). Small shrub with shoots of aromatic, silvery-white, woolly foliage with button-like yellow flowers in July and August. *S. chamaecyparissus* var. *nana* is a much more compact form. *S. pinnata* subsp. *neapolitana* (to 45 cm/18 in). The foliage is slightly greener, hairless and more softly ferny than *S. chamaecyparissus*. 'Edward Bowles' is a lovely form with creamy-yellow flowers. Full sun, well-drained, sandy soil. Propagate by softwood cuttings in early summer or semi-ripe

*Santolina chamaecyparissus*

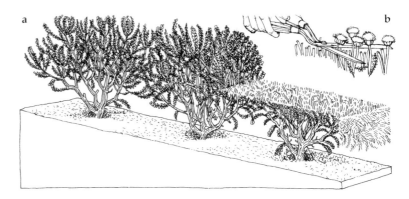

Trimming a santolina hedge (**a**). Clip the blooms away from flowering hedges with shears for a more formal look (**b**).

cuttings in early autumn. Sarah finds that *S. pinnata* subsp. *neapolitana,* as a more vigorous plant, can be slightly harder to manage within a tightly controlled design and feels that *S. chamaecyparissus* or the dwarf var. *nana* are the best formal hedging options. She has, however, experienced considerable confusion in naming within the nursery trade and advises that it is important to be clear on the foliage differences, since mistakes could ruin your grand schemes! 'I usually cut the santolinas back by about half at Easter time, to avoid damage of the young growth by late frosts as well as to keep them tidy and producing fresh growth from the base. There always comes a time, however, when they are too 'leggy' and woody to rapidly regenerate new shoots. Then you replace. For a very neat, formal hedge throughout the season, the flowers should be removed with shears.' **Uses** A medicinal herb which was once used to treat worms in children, but is now more valued as an insect repellant or simple ornamental.

**Lavendula 'Munstead'** To 45 cm (18 in). A compact, dark violet-flowered form of *L. angustifolia* or English lavender (syn. *L. spica*, *L. officinalis*). There are many lavender cultivars and choice depends on the effect you want to achieve (see Beningbrough Hall, p.61). 'I have considered replacing the central rosemaries with a taller lavender, since I quite like the idea of continuing the 'blocky' look of first santolina, then 'Hidcote' with a final peak of lavender in a different colour. The lavenders are trimmed back by about half at the same time as the santolina, but never into the oldest wood from which they would not readily regenerate. They are also deadheaded after flowering in order to prevent self-sown seedlings. Sarah has occasionally used hedge trimmers to trim the lavenders after flowering due to lack of time and liked the neat shape she achieved – much more formal than the shears she normally uses. It is important to do this as soon as possible after flowering, however, since any late summer trimming promotes new growth which is vulnerable to frost damage.

In very cold gardens it may be wiser to leave the seedheads on the plants over winter until the spring trimming since they will offer the plants additional winter protection.

### Design tips for herbs

● Gardening with herbs ornamentally is a game of playing with shapes and patterns. Try out your ideas for colour by comparing a bouquet of clippings from different herbs before you plant, just as if you were planning to redecorate a room.

● 'I am fond of seeing plants with a similar habit, but subtle colour differences growing together,' Sarah says. 'You don't have to achieve contrasty effect for the garden to be interesting. For instance, you could juxtapose block plantings of different cultivars and use those of different heights and flower colours, changing from white or pale mauve through to intense violet-blue.'

● Use a dark backdrop – like the hedge at Castle Drogo – to emphasise the strong shapes of tall architectural herbs such as lovage, cardoon and angelica.

● 'We have the shrub *Viburnum farreri* in the centre of our herb borders here, but you could use a herbaceous plant to give height during summer. Try the bronze or green forms of fennel (*Foeniculum vulgare*), depending on your colour scheme. But remember to remove the flower heads before they seed because self-sown seedlings can be difficult to shift.'

● If you want to grow herbs ornamentally there are many which you can scavenge from ornamental borders for cooking without damaging the display – including sage, rosemary, thyme, fennel, winter savory and marjoram. Most respond with nice fresh young growth if you pinch shoots for the pot. For harvesting large quantities of, for example, chives, parsley, basil or lavender flowers, you definitely need a purely productive herb patch, or grow herbs for culinary use in pots.

### Sarah's favourite herbs

**Welsh Onions or 'Ciboule' (*Allium fistulosum*)** 45-75cm (18-30in). Related to the Japanese bunching onions, which are an improved form of the traditional Welsh onion. Clump-forming, with swollen, bulb-like stem bases and may be used for edging in the same way as chives although, with white rather than purple drumstick flowers, a little more subdued in colouring. Sun or part shade. Self-sows readily or may be lifted, divided and replanted about 20cm (8in) apart in spring. In very cold areas they may require to be treated as annuals and sown in spring. **Uses** The small bulbous stem bases can be thinly sliced or the leaves chopped like chives.

Welsh Onion

LEFT: Fennel, sage and chives in the Herb Garden at Castle Drogo.

RIGHT: Egyptian tree onion (*Allium cepa* Proliferum Group)

**Egyptian Tree Onion (*Allium cepa* Proliferum Group)** To 90cm (36in). Hardier than the Welsh onions but may be used in the same way. The plants carry funny little bulbils on the stems after the white flowers have faded, before bending over and sprouting roots from each bulbil to multiply themselves. The bulbils may be used in cooking, or planted at 25cm (10in) spacings to produce new plants.

**Variegated Dwarf Comfrey (*Symphytum grandiflorum* 'Variegatum')** To 15cm (6in). A compact ornamental cousin to the more common medicinal comfrey, *Symphytum officinale* (see Gunby Hall, p.27). Pretty cream margins to the bristly leaves with tubular, creamy-white flowers in spring. Rich, moisture-retentive soil in part or full shade. Sun tends to scorch the creamy leaf margins. Propagate by division in autumn or spring. **Uses** Makes excellent groundcover, but will not produce the volume of foliage required for composting and comfrey fertilisers. For larger borders – and more foliage – the variegated Russian comfrey, *Symphytum* × *uplandicum* 'Variegatum', growing to 1m (3ft) is a good choice.

## Tips for using herbs

● **Sage gargle** To ease a sore throat or cough, infuse one teaspoon of fresh leaves in a cup of boiling water for ten minutes, then strain. Add one teaspoon of vinegar and gargle with the infusion. A sage 'tisane' or tea may be made in the same way, but without the vinegar.

● **Sweet cicely seeds** Nibble them fresh when they are still green, almost like a healthy sweet. Alternatively, allow the seeds to ripen on the plant before spreading on a tray to dry out, then pulverise them as they are too hard to use whole and add to soups, salads and cabbage or root vegetable dishes.

# Sissinghurst Castle

KENT

Area: 2·4 ha (6 acres)
Soil: Clay, neutral
Altitude: 61 m (200 ft)
Average rainfall: 737 mm (29 in)
Average climate: Moderate to
 cold winters with snow;
 hot, dry summers

There are few gardens whose story has been described and analysed to the extent that has been Sissinghurst's fate. So much of the thought and creative impulse of Vita Sackville-West and Harold Nicolson has enriched twentieth century gardening style – not just through the stream of visitors to the castle which has grown relentlessly since the first public opening in May 1938, but also through Vita's own reflections, published in her regular column for the *Observer*.

The Herb Garden was never intended for serious culinary purposes – while Vita and Harold were alive, there was a separate herb border for the use of their cook. Vita had a long-standing interest in the history, folklore and general air of mystery and romance surrounding the plants. The first steps towards a dedicated herb garden were taken when the surrounding yew hedge was planted in 1934 and her first herbs were established in the four original beds during 1938. In the course of the garden's restoration after the war years, the area was further subdivided with small paths and the simple pattern of twenty beds which we see today.

SARAH COOK trained at the Royal Botanic Gardens, Kew, and has led the staff of seven at Sissinghurst since 1991. The intensively gardened style which is one of Sissinghurst's hallmarks demands a consistent and intelligent horticultural input to each garden 'room'. Jacqui Ruthven cares for the Herb Garden, keeping a daily eye on its progress and, in tandem with Sarah, makes any necessary improvements. 'I enjoy the way in which I have the opportunity to experiment with the small, intimate plant associations in the Herb Garden,' she says. 'But I'm not one of those people who can reel off herbal folklore at the drop of a hat. I think you have to be a herbalist to do that with confidence. People shouldn't mess about with plants if they are unsure what they are doing – some are quite safe, but others are really very dangerous.'

## Herbs at Sissinghurst

The herbs are tucked away in the south-east corner of the garden, a formal seclusion behind high yew hedging which seems a little out of keeping with the increasingly informal plantings as one moves from the Tower and walled court-yards. 'We try to avoid having anything which is purely ornamental in here – everything has to have a use,' says Jacqui. 'But sometimes the uses are fairly tenuous – we want the garden to look good, after all!' Many cottage garden flowers

creep into the Herb Garden under the guise of salad or vegetable crops, but the gardeners are always careful to select
the most ornamental cultivars. Hence the choice of beautiful
deep red nasturtium 'Empress of India' with dark, pea-green
foliage, to represent the race whose leaves may be used in
salads while the seed pods are pickled as capers. Or the young
shoots of bistort (*Persicaria*), eaten as an asparagus replacement in the same way as hops, and represented here by the
ornamental, fluffy pink pokers of *Persicara bistorta* 'Superba'.

## Gardening with annual and biennial herbs

The Herb Garden at Sissinghurst contains a far higher propor-
tion of annual and biennial herbs than many other parts of the
herb garden. Sarah and Jacqui therefore have a number of
strategies to ensure that they have a steady supply of replacement herbs to fill unsightly border gaps. 'There is no main
planting season.' Jacqui says. 'I find that throughout the
summer I am planting two or three varieties out each week.'

● Most of the annual and biennial herbs are sown in containers in the green-houses, then pricked out into individual pots.
Once growing strongly, some biennials are grown on in nursery rows until they are required to fill gaps. Many annuals
– like coriander, chervil and dill – resent root disturbance so
are sown into plug trays and potted on to minimise root
damage.

● All the seeds are sown into a soil-based John Innes Seed
compost. Hardy dill would be sown in March in plug trays
in a cold greenhouse. Two to four seeds are sown to each cell
and the seedlings are not thinned but potted on in their
clumps into 7·5 cm (3 in) pots. Tender annuals such as basil are
sown in temperatures of 15-20°C (59-68°F) to aid germination
and are never planted out before the end of May.

● Jacqui increasingly solves the 'summer gap' problem by
sowing biennials like evening primrose, verbascum, teasel
and clary early – perhaps in May rather than June. When gaps
appear, large young biennials are on hand to fill them.

● She also keeps an eye on perennial plants whose position
she wants to rotate. If annuals and biennials such as borage
are past their best by July, she will fill the gap with the perennial which is due for rotation. For a short time she will have
two plantings of the same herb – but no gaps!

## Pruning and replacing herbs

'People don't like to keep on cutting plants down or taking
them out completely,' says Jacqui 'But when you garden with
herbs in Britain this is absolutely essential'.

Basil, parsley and thyme
arranged in pots.

Pruning sage.

Cutting artemisia back to its woody mounded base.

At Sissinghurst, lavender is carefully dead-headed by hand.

● **Sage** 'I clip our sages very hard back each year in March, just into the old wood which will then re-shoot. I expect to have to replace them every three or four years, since an older plant would just pack up if you tried to do that to it. Just keep cutting back shrubby herbs as long as they will take it – but make sure you use the clippings to propagate!'

● **Artemisia** The top growth of *Artemisia abrotanum* (southernwood) and *A. absinthium* (wormwood) is cut back by half in autumn and then further back to a woody base in March. The top growth supplies the root system with a little frost protection over the winter, while the hard pruning ensures that the plant renews itself with healthy growth in spring. The plants have an indefinite lifespan of five to ten years.

● **Hyssop, winter savory** These are deadheaded in autumn and then, as for the artemisia, pruned hard back in March. These have a life expectancy of five to seven years.

● **Deadheading lavender** Lavender at Sissinghurst is not clipped as such, but deadheaded very carefully by hand or with secateurs directly after flowering, since the gardeners feel the plants respond better to this treatment. 'If you have the time to take them back very carefully by hand, you can get back to a nice young shoot every time,' Jacqui says. 'Trimming the whole plant with shears doesn't produce such uniform regrowth. We never shear them in spring either.'

## Cultivating herbs in containers

The low, fine-textured thyme in the marble bowl at the centre of the garden is complemented by the foliage of containerised herbs elsewhere. 'Generally we put three pots of herbs next to the camomile seat and then we finish off a few of the little paths which run out from the main axes with an occasional group – but we try not to overdo it', Jacqui says.

● Growing herbs in pots gives you the flexibility to re-create the sharp drainage and hot conditions which many enjoy in the wild – and the option of returning them to the greenhouse in rain. Basil particularly benefits from this treatment.

● At Sissinghurst, a variety of clay pots and shallow pans are used, although 30 cm (12 in) is the most common size. The final display is therefore made more interesting by gradations in height and size in addition to their contrasting foliage.

● All the pot-grown herbs are planted in a loam-based, John Innes No. 2 compost with additional grit. The base of each pot is crocked with broken pot shards, to improve drainage.

● Tender perennials like lemon grass and thyme will be overwintered in a frost-free greenhouse.

The Herb Garden ablaze with colour at Sissinghurst Castle.

● The pots are generally given a dilute liquid feed once a fortnight and checked for watering every other day. It is important to adjust watering to suit the plant: thyme likes dry conditions, but heat-loving basil needs plenty of water to keep the foliage lush. Under-watering basil tends to promote flowering with subsequent reduction in the flavour of the foliage.

## Sissinghurst favourites for containers

**Lemon Grass (*Cymbopogon citratus*)** 1·5 m (5 ft). An aromatic grass from tropical and warm temperate regions which forms vigorous tall clumps, sometimes with almost bamboo-like stems, and produces plenty of graceful, lemon-scented foliage. Rarely flowers in cultivation. A decorative perennial grass for containers. Overwinter in a greenhouse or conservatory at a minimum temperature of 7–10°C (45–50°F). Pot into very well-drained, loam-based compost incorporating a slow-release fertiliser. Divide in spring to propagate and repot into fresh compost annually. **Uses** Used internally to treat digestive and feverish complaints in children and externally against lice, ringworm and athlete's foot.

**Basil (*Ocimum basilicum*)** To 60cm (24in). The familiar, softly succulent, aromatic green leaves of annual basil have long been an essential element in Italian cuisine, but there are many variants, showing differences in leaf form, colouring and flavour. Green-leaved 'Genovese' is acknowledged as the best for pesto sauces and sweet flavoured curly basil, *O. basilicum* var. *crispum,* (syn. 'Neapolitano') is an excellent all-round culinary form. Purple forms such as 'Dark Opal' and the frilly leaves of 'Purple Ruffles' are highly ornamental as well as useful in cooking, while the citrus flavours of lemon basil, *O. basilicum* var. *citriodorum,* associate well with herb vinegars and fish dishes. Demands summer warmth and sunlight to maximise production of the volatile oils. Pinch young plants to promote bushiness when they are about 10-15cm (4-6in) high and then pinch plants regularly to keep them bushy. (See Hardwick Hall, p.39, for tips on seed sowing.) **Uses** Primarily a culinary herb, but the oil is used by aromatherapists and the leaves, seeds and oils have been used medicinally: internally to treat feverish colds, depression and exhaustion; externally against acne, skin infections and bites or stings.

### Planting and maintaining a camomile seat
On the north-facing side of the garden is a low camomile seat, constructed from old masonry. The centre is hollow and filled with rubble at the base. At the surface a 50:50 mixture of garden soil and compost provides sharp drainage conditions. The soil is replaced once every two or three years, but the camomile is completely replanted each spring. 'The camomile grows well and the seat is a lovely feature – but only with our help!' says Jackie. 'Each autumn we rip it to pieces and re-propagate for planting out in the following spring.'

Cross section of the camomile seat at Sissinghurst.

● The seat is quite small and takes twenty-five to thirty plants, which are spaced about 10cm (4in) apart.

● The camomile for the following season's seat is propagated each year in September and October using 'slips' or Irishman's cuttings. Each small portion is planted up into a John Innes seed compost, using 7·5cm (3in) pots or plug trays, depending on the size of the root system.

● Overwinter in a frost-free greenhouse or cold frame for planting out the following March.

● After planting, the seat is watered thoroughly and then checked regularly during the summer – it must not be allowed to dry out completely. No fertiliser is used.

## Jacqui's favourite herbs

**Chervil (*Anthriscus cerefolium*)** To 30cm (12in) or more. Umbels of tiny white flowers in early summer. Hardy annual with bright green, lacy leaves, tasting slightly of aniseed and resembling a diminutive plain-leaved (French, Italian) parsley. Plant in well-drained, but moisture-retentive soil in part to full shade. An ideal container herb for a shady position, provided it is frequently watered. Propagate from seed sown in March or April and sow in succession until the autumn, either directly into the open ground, thinning to 10-20cm (4–8in), or in cell modules and pots. Avoid pricking out, since both root disturbance and dry summer conditions cause plants to run to seed with a consequent reduction in leaf quality. Plants may be grown under glass or polythene protection for a winter crop. Seeds rapidly lose their germination power. **Uses** Although a popular medicinal herb in the Middle Ages and still used by herbalists today to treat circulatory or urinary disorders and to soothe inflamed eyes, the modern uses of chervil are predominantly culinary – chop into salads or add to potato, fish and egg dishes just before serving. Use fresh or freeze as chervil does not dry well.

**Coriander (*Coriandrum sativum*)** To 70cm (28in). Umbels of small white to mauve flowers in summer. A hardy annual, with a pungent aroma, coriander has light green, lobed leaves which become more finely divided on flowering plants. Like chervil, it runs rapidly to seed, especially if plants dry out at the seedling stage. Sow as for chervil in a sunny position on light, well-drained soil, although plants grown in semi-shade produce good foliage for culinary use. **Uses** Internally for digestive problems; externally to treat haemorrhoids and painful joints. The Romans used it as a meat preservative and in the Middle Ages it was even mixed with love potions for its supposed aphrodisiac qualities.

Coriander

Dill

**Dill (*Anethum graveolens*)** 60-90cm (24-36in). Umbels of yellow flowers in late summer and soft green, feathery foliage resembling fennel, but with a sweeter, more delicate scent. The flowers attract hoverflies which feed on aphids, making this a useful companion plant. Hardy annual which prefers a warm, sunny position on light, well-drained soil and tolerates slightly acidic conditions. Sow in succession as for chervil and thin to 20cm (8in). May run prematurely to seed if over-crowded or growing in dry conditions. The tastiest foliage is produced just before flowering. **Uses** An important medicinal herb since Biblical times, dill has been used for digestive disorders including colic and wind in babies. Dill leaves lose their flavour when cooked for long, so should be used fresh as a garnish, or added to sauces just before serving.

**Summer Savory (*Satureja hortensis*)** 10-38cm (4-15in). Small leafy clusters of white, pink or lilac flowers in summer. Summer savory is a half-hardy annual which produces one widely branching stem clothed in small, narrow leaves with a hot, spicy scent. A good bee plant, it prefers a warm, sunny position on light, preferably alkaline, soil. Sow in late April, thinning to 15cm (6in) apart and pinch the young shoots to encourage bushiness. Entire plants may be uprooted and dried in bunches for winter use. **Uses** Although primarily of culinary value, summer savory has an ancient reputation as an aphrodisiac and has also been used medicinally to treat indigestion and wind, but is never given to pregnant women. Jacqui finds it adds a hot peppery 'bite' to green salads and works well in pulse and bean dishes, sausages and stuffings.

## Tips for using herbs

● **Pesto sauce** Take 15g (½oz) of fresh basil leaves, 1 crushed garlic clove, a pinch of salt, 50g (2oz) pine nuts, 4 tablespoons of fresh, grated parmesan and 6 tablespoons of olive oil. Whizz the basil leaves round in a food processor, then add all the ingredients except the olive oil and mix. Transfer the paste to a saucepan and gradually stir in the olive oil heating gently.

● **Harvest coriander seeds** in August when they have turned from green to grey on the plants and they smell pleasantly aromatic. Dry the seeds – still on their stalks – in a warm, dry shed for a few days. Then clean them by alternately threshing, sieving and blowing the stems and debris away. Store the seeds in an air-tight jar – the aroma improves with time.

# Barrington Court

SOMERSET

Area: 4·5 ha (11 acres)
Soil: Fertile loam over clay;
   neutral to slightly alkaline
Altitude: 20 m (65 ft)
Average rainfall: 762 mm (30 in)
Average climate: Mild, wet
   winters; warm, relatively
   dry summers

When the National Trust acquired the sixteenth-century manor house of Barrington Court in Somerset at the beginning of the twentieth century, it was graceful but crumbling, with one wing inhabited by a farmer, the rest left to owls and chickens, and no garden to speak of. The series of intimate Elizabethan-style walled gardens which we enjoy today was conceived by the architect J. E. Forbes and garden designer Gertrude Jekyll, thanks to the vision and enthusiasm of the Lyle family – tenants of the Trust between 1920 and 1991.

The walls which surround all Barrington's garden rooms provide a valuable source of warmth and protection for shrubby Mediterranean herbs. The huge, open kitchen garden is the largest room of all, and the site selected for the culinary herbs is sheltered against the warmest, south-west facing wall where wall-trained apricots also benefit from the heat.

CHRISTINE BRAIN trained at Cannington College in Somerset and has been Head Gardener leading a staff of three at Barrington Court since 1978. Her approach to herbs is very in tune with the garden itself. 'I wouldn't say I am particularly fond of herbs as such – herbaceous plants are my real love.' But silvery artemisia, soft purple sage and lavender are very much keynote plants in the garden and any gardener using them in such an inspired way might be inclined to disregard practical medicinal or household use. For Christine their gentle form, pastel foliage colours and evocative scent are integral to Barrington's style and it would be hard to imagine gardening here without them.

## Herbs at Barrington

The repetitive use of herbs such as catmint, purple sage and *Artemisia* spp. is a very distinctive feature of Jekyll's style. Surely one of the reasons for her fond and frequent use of these particular plants must have been the way in which their leaf textures and gentle shapes softened and contrasted with the paving materials which are such a feature of the gardens over whose design she collaborated. The long, flowing 'sausages' of her designs ensure that each planting group appears to weave its way through companions towards the observer. Moreover, colours are never seen in isolation or in one to one combinations, but as a much more complicated symphony of many diverse elements blended at each viewpoint.

The Rose and Iris Garden at Barrington Court is a perfect example of this successful strategy, showing how Jekyll used her herbal favourites, in this case purple sage (*Salvia officin-alis* 'Purpurascens') and the ornamental catmint (*Nepeta* × *faassenii*). Many different iris cultivars are planted in winding ribbons in the outer borders so that they snake their way through adjoining plants. Visually, there appears to be no beginning and end to each group. Their diversity of colour is brought together and harmonised by similar ribbons of soft purple sage or fringes of grey catmint which are repeated around the four sides of the garden.

'There are probably thirty or forty purple sages in the Rose and Iris Garden', Christine says, 'planted in company with *Echinops ritro*, phlox and iris. It really is rather lovely with the dome shape of the sage and the very upright irises contrasting. But we are continually replanting and propagating because the sages are so short-lived. I think that regular propagation is probably almost the most important element in successful herb gardening – whether decorative or utilitarian.'

### Favourite Barrington Court foliage herbs

**Catmint (*Nepeta cataria*)** 40-100cm (16-40in). Highly aromatic herbaceous perennial with woolly stems and small, heart-shaped; coarsely toothed, grey-green leaves, almost white on the under surface. Small white or pink flowers are carried in the leaf axils in mid-summer. This is the wild form of catmint, so popular with cats for its powerful scent which is said to be similar to pheromones given off by cats of the opposite sex – a cat aphrodisiac, in fact! Gertrude Jekyll favoured 'garden catmint', *Nepeta* × *faassenii* (syn. *N. mussini* of gardens), a popular edging plant with pretty purple-blue flowers and recommended clipping it over just after flowering for a new flush of bloom in August. Both species like well-drained, but moisture-retentive soil in full sun. Propagate from seed or by division in spring. Leave top growth on plants over winter until the following April to protect the root system in cold weather. **Uses** Wild catmint attracts bees as well as cats. Medicinally it has been used to treat fevers, colds, digestive disorders and to promote sleep. Used to flavour salads, as a mint-like tea – and to stuff catnip mice!

**Wormwoods, Sage Brushes (*Artemisia* spp.)** These relatives of tarragon are amongst the bitterest of herbs, with a range of medicinal and household uses. The Latin name means 'without sweetness', while the word 'wormwood' comes from the German 'Wermut', or 'preserver of the mind', since true wormwood, *Artemisia absinthium*, was thought to boost brain activity. The finely divided, silver or grey-green, semi-evergreen foliage of many is of great ornamental value in the herbaceous or mixed border. The flowers are usually yellow or

Catmint

white, carried close on the stems or in small spikes at the stem tips but are only truly decorative in a few species. Plant in spring in light, well-drained, preferably neutral to alkaline soil in full sun. *A. lactiflora* prefers moist, neutral to acid soil and grows in part-shade. Some species are less than completely hardy, particularly on heavy, poorly drained soil. Propagate shrubs and sub-shrubs such as *A. absinthium* and *A. arborescens* by semi-ripe cuttings in late summer, herbaceous perennials by division in spring. Clip shrubs hard back in March or April to young shoots visible on the basal wood.

**Southernwood, Lad's Love, Old Man (*A. abrotanum*)** To 3 ft (1 m). Hardy sub-shrub with very fine, feathery, grey-green leaves. **Uses** For centuries an effective insect repellant and used from Tudor times in herbal posies or 'tussie-mussies' to ward off noxious smells and infection in the street. Also an old cure for baldness. Used medicinally for delayed or painful menstruation, poor appetite or digestion, as well as threadworms in children, but never given to pregnant women.

**Wormwood (*A. absinthium*)** To 1 m (3 ft). Sub-shrub with very deeply divided, grey-green leaves, silkily hairy on both sides. 'Lambrook Silver' and taller 'Lambrook Giant' are good ornamental cultivars with particularly fine silver foliage. Frost-hardy to −5°C (23°F) and very drought tolerant. **Uses** Used in absinthe until it was discovered to have hallucinogenic and addictive properties and to damage the nervous system. Used medicinally for digestive problems, gall bladder complaints, to treat roundworm and, externally, to treat bruises and bites. Never given to children or pregnant women.

**Tree Wormwood (*A. arborescens*)** To 1·1 m (3½ ft). Sub-shrub with finely divided silver foliage, more lacy and refined than other artemisias. Half-hardy, tolerating temperatures down to 0°C (32°F), so semi-ripe cuttings annually are advisable. Slightly less vigorous but hardier 'Powis Castle' is possibly a hybrid between this species and *A. absinthium* which produces no flowers. **Uses** Leaves used in herbal posies.

**Western Mugwort, Cudweed (*A. ludoviciana*)** 0·6-1·2 m (2-4 ft). Hardy herbaceous perennial with creeping, rhizomatous rootstock forming a mat of erect stems clothed in grey-green to silver, narrow, lance-shaped leaves. *A. ludoviciana* 'Silver Queen' has very ornamental silver foliage which is finely cut. Very drought tolerant. **Uses** Leaves used in herbal posies.

**Roman Wormwood, Small Absinthe (*A. pontica*)** 0·4-1·2 m (1½-4 ft). Hardy sub-shrub. The creeping, rhizomatous rootstock produces unbranched, erect stems covered in feathery grey-green leaves. Lovely silver foliage groundcover where

*Artemisia abisinthium* (TOP);
*A. ludoviciana* (CENTRE);
*A. arborescens* (BOTTOM).

the invasive habit does not threaten companions. **Uses** For flavouring wine and absinthe.

**Mugwort (*A. vulgaris*)** 0·6-1·7m (2-5¹/₂ft). Vigorously spreading hardy herbaceous perennial with dark green, divided leaves, clothed with white hairs on the undersurface. **Uses** Known as 'mother of herbs', mugwort was associated with witchcraft or fertility rites and used by both the Druids and Anglo-Saxons. The common name may refer to its use in flavouring beer before the use of hops. Medicinally to encourage menstruation, or to treat depression, loss of appetite and roundworms. Not given to pregnant or lactating women.

### Propagating grey-leaved herbs from semi-ripe cuttings

Many sun-loving herbs such as wormwoods, sage, lavender and curry plant have a dense clothing of small hairs on either or both sides of the leaf surface – it is this that gives them their silver or grey colouring. This silky layer helps the plants survive in the very dry Mediterranean climates where they frequently grow wild: the hairs trap moisture and help protect the plant from excessive water loss. What benefits plants in the wild can be a problem when taking cuttings or over-wintering the plants in the average British winter, since the foliage is prone to rot in the humid conditions of a propagating frame. Christine has a number of tricks to ensure that the cuttings survive and root. Many grey-leaved shrubs and sub-shrubs are rooted from 'heel' cuttings since the small 'heel' of ripened wood helps protect against rot (see Bateman's p.22).

● Christine is always very careful to remove any untidy snags or leaf debris from the base of grey-leaved cuttings with a sharp knife. Trays of cuttings growing on in cold frames are also checked over and tidied of rotting leaves regularly. 'Tidiness and hygiene are particularly important with the greys, since anything which can rot, will rot!' she says.

● The cuttings are inserted in seed trays. For grey-leaved subjects she often substitutes perlite in varying quantities for the sharp sand of the standard 50:50 peat and sharp sand mix used for the late summer cuttings of penstemon, diascia, argyranthemum or osteospermum. 'We have to arrive at a much coarser, sharply drained compost for some of the greys,' she says. 'Southernwood, which roots quite easily, might go into 50:50 peat and perlite, but for plants which are more prone to rot – such as unusual artemisias like *A. caucasica* – I might use pure perlite. And then, of course, there are the different stages in between. We simply have to judge the situation according to previous experience. A very white or

OPPOSITE: Marjoram, Welsh onions and lovage in the Kitchen Garden at Barrington Court.

Dusting the base of a grey-leaved cutting with hormone rooting powder.

woolly leaf is a strong hint that you might experience problems. However, sharply drained mixtures tend to dry out more quickly and must be regularly checked for watering.'

● Hormone rooting powder is used sparingly in propagation at Barrington Court and grey-leaved subjects would be the most likely cuttings to receive a light dusting at the base before insertion in the rooting medium. 'Hormone rooting powder has to be very fresh to be effective,' says Christine. 'I use it for the fungicide it contains rather than for its ability to enhance root formation. It helps stop the base of the grey foliage cuttings from rotting before they produce new roots.'

● The cold frames have heating cables laid to run through the sand base. The temperature of the base on which the cuttings stand in their trays will therefore be about 15°C (60°F), but the air above can still freeze and so it is important that the frames are kept closed during cold weather.

● The grey-leaved herbs are kept separately in the frames from green-leaved plants. In this way, Christine can keep a slightly drier atmosphere in the grey-leaved frame.

● Sometimes, if she is propagating herbs which she has found prone to rot such as the felty-leaved relative of common southernwood, *A. stelleriana,* she covers the compost surface with a layer of grit or sharp sand after inserting the cuttings, to keep the foliage off the moist surface.

● The cold frames are generally closed after the cuttings have been taken, but Christine tries to prevent the cuttings from sweating. Depending on the weather – and most frequently in warm, dry weather during early autumn – she will often vent the cold frames for an hour or so each day, to allow excess condensation to dry on the foliage and glass.

● If the cuttings are well-rooted by October, she will pot them on into individual 9cm (3¹/₂in) pots of a very sharply drained John Innes No. 2 type mix to which she has added an extra part of horticultural grit. Cuttings which are not well-rooted are left for potting until February. 'November and December are terrible months for plant growth and if you pot poorly rooted cuttings then they will just sit and rot in their pots.' The cuttings are set out to grow on in the greenhouse, kept at a minimum temperature of 2°C (36°F) until planting in April.

● Lavender or purple-leaved sage are sometimes lined out in the vegetable garden for use as stock plants since cutting material from younger plants yields the highest success rate. 'When you use as many of these little short-lived shrubs as we do here, its important always to have replacement plants growing on behind the scenes,' Christine comments.

## Tips for planting culinary herbs

Culinary herbs are treated in much the same way as a vegetable crop at Barrington, since during their short season of growth, the aim will be to encourage as much fresh foliage for cutting as possible. 'Dill, chervil and parsley are all cultivated on a richer diet here than the majority of herbs,' says Christine.

● Christine finds it impossible to sow annuals directly into the open ground at Barrington because the weed competition in March is fierce. 'We raise them in plug trays and plant them out in April, in a sunny area when the soil is beginning to warm up. We use a soil-based John Innes seed compost.'

● Christine describes the soil as quite hungry, requiring farmyard manure annually to enrich it for vegetables. The ground where annual herbs are grown is dug and manured during early winter in the same way.

● A light dressing of a balanced fertiliser is forked lightly into the soil at planting time.

● Care is taken over watering, as with all vegetables. Elsewhere in the garden, ornamental herbs will be watered carefully during establishment, but rarely irrigated thereafter.

● Parsley is often sown very early in February with bottom heat of approximately 15°C (60°F), pricked out individually into 6.25 cm (2½ in) pots. When planted out in March, the young foliage is protected with cloches.

## Christine's favourite herbs

**Parsley (*Petroselinum crispum*)** A biennial herb, usually grown as an annual, and too commonly cultivated for its crispy, nutritious foliage to require description. Many gardeners agree that the plain, flat-leaved or French parsley has a far superior flavour to the common 'curly' variety. Christine likes to grow the variety 'Moss Curled' as well as the plain-leaved each season. Myths have grown up around parsley's notoriously slow germination rate. It is said to go down to the Devil and back several times before germination and will only grow in a household where the woman is master! For cultivation tips and sowing technique, see also Gunby Hall, p.30, and Hardwick Hall, p.39. **Uses** The Romans wore garlands of the herb at feasts to prevent intoxication, but it has also been used as a lotion to treat insect bites and the juice is an effective insect repellent. Also used to treat cystitis, anorexia and irregular menstrual cycles, but should not be taken by pregnant women or those suffering from kidney disease. Also said to be good for treating eye infections, preventing hair loss and making freckles vanish! Chewing a few leaves helps to counteract the smell of a garlicky meal.

Parsley

Chives

**Chives (*Allium schoenoprasum*)** To 15cm (6in) when not in flower. This onion relative is one of the staples in the herb gardener's culinary repertoire. Chives are a perennial bulbous herb, but the clumps of bulbs are best divided every two to three years in spring or autumn and replanted into rich, moisture-retentive soil in full sun or part-shade. They require plenty of moisture in dry weather to produce good foliage for cutting. Easily raised from seed sown in spring. Sow seed in small clumps in cell modules and, when these are growing strongly, transfer them to the open ground at 23cm (9in) spacings. Flowering chives produce hollow stems which are useless in the kitchen and as soon as the flowers have gone over, plants should be cut hard back so that they produce a fresh flush of growth for use. Cutting chives for the kitchen always stimulates regrowth and they tolerate cutting back several times in the course of a season. Chives die back in winter, but cloching clumps in February or March produces very early, kitchen-ready growth. **Uses** The common name derives from the Latin 'cepa' or onion. A substitute for spring onions, although they have a special flavour of their own, chives make a particularly good garnish for potato or egg dishes. Use the little purple flowers individually, breaking the flowerheads up, to add bite and colour to green salads.

## Tips for using herbs

● **Moth bags** Southernwood and mugwort make effective moth repellants for wardrobes and cupboards. Mix a handful each of dried southernwood, mugwort, thyme and tansy, then add a tablespoon of crushed cloves or coriander to extend the active life of the herbs. Cut small pieces of thin cotton or muslin to the required size and stitch them together before stuffing with the herb mixture. Even a bag 7.5cm (3in) square would be suitable to protect stored blankets or woollens from moth damage, although several of these would be required for a drawerful of clothing. The scent which the herbs leave on materials is pleasant, unlike that of camphorated moth balls.

● **Freezing soft-leaved annual herbs such as dill, chervil, basil and tarragon** The flavour of these is better preserved by freezing rather than drying. Pick them in small sprays, chop the leaves, fill ice cube trays and pour over a little water. Melt the ice cubes as you require the herbs. Alternatively, pick the herbs and tear or crumble them up with your fingers, then freeze without water in small plastic, lidded containers.

# Plant Directory

## Perennial Herbs

### For full sun only

**Catmint/Catnip** (*Nepeta cataria*, **Lamiaceae**) See Barrington Court p.80

**Camomile** (*Chamaemelum nobile* **syn.** *Anthemis nobilis*, **Asteraceae**) See Springhill p.45

**Chinese or Garlic Chives** (*Allium tuberosum*, **Alliaceae**) To 50cm (20in). This rhizomatous perennial related to onions and chives carries small, white heads of sweet-scented, onion-like flowers in late summer. Grow in much the same way as chives, although prefers full sun. Propagate from seed in spring or by division in autumn and spring. **Uses** Medicinally for bladder and kidney complaints. The foliage and flowers both have a mild, garlic taste which is excellent in salads.

**Cotton Lavender** (*Santolina* **spp.**, **Asteraceae**) See Castle Drogo p.67

**Curry Plant** (*Helichrysum italicum* **syn.** *H. angustifolium*, **Asteraceae**) See Bateman's, p.24

**Dyer's Camomile** (*Anthemis tinctoria*, **Asteraceae**) See Castle Drogo, p.66

**Egyptian Tree Onion** (*Allium cepa* **Proliferum Group**, **Alliaceae**) See Castle Drogo, p.71

**Fennel** (*Foeniculum vulgare*, **Apiaceae**) See Bateman's, p.23

**Garlic** (*Allium sativum*, **Alliaceae**) 30-120cm (12-48in), with white, onion-like flowerheads in June and July. Requires a long growing season and a cold period of one or two months for a good crop. Plant healthy-looking bulbs which are guaranteed virus and nematode-free in late autumn. Best on light, well-drained alkaline soil, manured for the previous crop, but may be planted on ridges on heavy soils. Break up bulbs into individual cloves and plant at at least twice the depth of the clove with the flat base of each down. Space cloves 18cm (7in) apart each way in blocks or plant in rows 25-30cm (10-12in) apart, with 7.5-10cm (3-4in) between the cloves. Keep weed-free but do not feed. Lift for drying when the leaves fade and turn yellow. **Uses** Valued for centuries for its antiseptic and antibiotic properties, the juice was applied to soldiers' wounds in the First World War. A general aid to health if eaten regularly, it is used medicinally to treat bronchitis and gastroenteritis and can lower high blood pressure and regulate blood glucose levels. The cloves are commonly used in cooking, but in the East it is also cultivated for the young shoots and flowering heads.

**Hyssop** (*Hyssopus officinalis*, **Lamiaceae**) See Buckland Abbey, p.53

**Lavender** (*Lavandula* **spp.**, **Lamiaceae**) See Beningbrough Hall, p.60

**Marsh Mallow** (*Althaea officinalis*, **Malvaceae**) 1-1.2m (3-4ft). Softly hairy perennial related to hollyhock, with large, velvety leaves and pale pink flowers in summer. A tall plant which usefully thrives on very heavy clay or waterlogged soil. Propagate by division in autumn or by seed in late summer. **Uses** Often associated with the old-fashioned throat lozenges made from the powdered roots, the Latin name for marsh mallow comes from the Greek word 'to cure'. Also used for treating cystitis, sore eyes, sprains, bruises and abscesses.

**Marjorams, Pot and Wild** (*Origanum onites*, *O. vulgare*, **Lamiaceae**) See Gunby Hall, p.31

**Mugworts** (*Artemisia vulgaris*, **Asteraceae**) See Barrington Court, p.82

**Mullein, Aaron's Rod** (*Verbascum thapsus*, **Scrophulariaceae**) See Buckland Abbey, p.54

**Myrtle** (*Myrtus communis*, **Myrtaceae**) To 3m (10ft), with fragrant white flowers in spring and summer, followed by black berries. The small, oval, shiny leaves of this upright, evergreen shub have a juniper like scent when crushed. A charming structural plant for the winter herb garden, but will only survive temperatures down to about -10°c (14°F), and demands a sunny position, sheltered from cold wind. Plant in spring on well-drained, neutral to alkaline soil. Prune back winter-damaged growth in March/April. Propagate from seed in spring or semi-ripe cuttings in summer, rooted in a closed propagator with gentle bottom heat of about 15-20°c (59-68°F). **Uses** The oil is used in perfumery, soaps and skin preparations. Medicinally for urinary infections, sinusitis, and dry coughs. The leaves are used fresh in pork and lamb dishes and the fruits (*mursin*) are used as a spice in the Middle East.

**Orris** (*Iris germanica* **var.** *florentina* **Iridaceae**) 0.6-1.2m (2-4ft). The beautiful white, violet-tinged flowers of this bearded iris appear in May while its typically sword-shaped leaves make an interesting contrast in form with the more rounded shapes of many herbs. Plant in spring in well-drained, neutral to alkaline soil. Divide the rhizomatous roots in July after flowering. **Uses** Grown even in classical times for the volatile violet-scented oil produced by the rhizomatous root. Dried roots are ground into a powder for use in perfumery, but orris has also been used to treat chest complaints and diarrhoea. In spite of its medicinal use, all parts of the plant – particularly the rhizomes – are harmful if eaten.

**Rosemary (*Rosmarinus officinalis*, Lamiaceae)** See Springhill, p.47

**Rue, Herb of Grace (*Ruta graveolens*, Rutaceae)** To 45cm (18in) or more, with small clusters of greenish-yellow flowers in July and August. The lobed, blue-green, rather lacy leaves of this small, bitterly aromatic, evergreen shrub, native to southern Europe, provide useful strong foliage colour in herb borders. Handle with caution as rue is a well-known skin irritant. Particularly ornamental are the cream-variegated rue, *R. graveolens* 'Variegata' and the fine, very blue-leaved form, 'Jackman's Blue'. Plant on well-drained, preferably poor, neutral to alkaline soil in spring. Cut winter-damaged rue back in spring. See Hardwick Hall, p.38, for tips on pruning. Propagate by semi-ripe cuttings in late summer. **Uses** The common name may originate from a Greek word, 'to set free', symbolising the belief that it could free the body of numerous ills. 'Herb of Grace' is thought to derive from the use of rue brushes to sprinkle holy water. An old antidote to many ills – including plague, poison and witches – it has also been used to treat sick cattle and to ward off fleas and insect infestations. Rue has abortive properties and is toxic in large doses and should only be taken under qualified supervision.

**Russian Tarragon (*Artemisia dracunculus*, Asteraceae)** See Hardwick Hall, p.37

**Sage (*Salvia officinalis*, Lamiaceae)** See Bateman's, p.21

**Southernwood (*Artemisia abrotanum*, Asteraceae)** See Barrington Court, p.81

**Thyme (*Thymus spp.*, Lamiaceae)** See Buckland Abbey, p.53

**Wall Germander (*Teucrium × lucidrys* syn. *T. chamaedrys*, Lamiaceae)** See Castle Drogo, p.66

**Welsh Onion (*Allium fistulosum*, Alliaceae)** See Castle Drogo, p.69

**Winter Savory (*Satureja montana*, Lamiaceae)** 15–40cm (6–16in). A small-leaved, stiff-stemmed aromatic sub-shrub, rather like thyme in appearance, and producing pale purple to pink flowers in June. Grow in sharply drained to dry soil, and plant in spring. Propagate from seed or by division in spring. **Uses** A pot herb, with uses similar to those of annual summer savory although it has a spicier flavour. Should not be taken when pregnant.

**Wormwoods (*Artemisia absinthium*, *A. arborescens*, *A. pontica*, Asteraceae)** See Barrington Court, p.80

## Sun or part-day shade

**Agrimony (*Agrimonia eupatoria*, Rosaceae)** 30–60cm (12–24in). An erect, downy and rather short-lived apricot-scented British native with divided leaves and long spikes of yellow flowers. Tolerates partial shade and dry soils, but happier in fertile, moist conditions. Plant in autumn or spring and sow seed or divide in spring. **Uses** An important wound herb in the Middle Ages, it has also been used to treat diarrhoea, rheumatism, food allergies, sore throats and conjunctivitis.

**Alecost, Costmary (*Tanacetum balsamita*, syn. *Balsamita major*, Asteraceae)** See Hardwick Hall, p.41

**Bay (*Laurus nobilis*, Lauraceae)** See Springhill, p.46

**Chives (*Allium schoenoprasum*, Alliaceae)** See Barrington Court, p.86

**Dandelion (*Taraxacum officinale*, Asteraceae)** 10–20cm (4–8in). While it is unlikely that the much-despised perennial dandelion will be deliberately cultivated in any garden other than that of a very serious herb collector, its medicinal uses go back too far to allow its exclusion here. **Uses** The Latin name derives from the Greek for 'eye disorders' and 'to cure'. In France, dandelion is known as *pissenlit*, roughly translated as 'wet-the-bed', alluding to its powerful diuretic properties. Modern herbalists recognise its value for degenerative joint diseases. The young, spring leaves are used in soups and salads; summer leaves and flowers for making dandelion wine and tea, and the roots as a coffee substitute.

**Elecampane (*Inula helenium*, Asteraceae)** See Buckland Abbey, p.55

**Feverfew (*Tanacetum parthenium*, syn. *Matricaria parthenium*, *Chrysanthemum parthenium*, Asteraceae)** To 60cm (24in). Perennial with small, rather chrysanthemum-like, pungently scented, lobed leaves and little branching heads of white, yellow-centred daisy flowers in summer. A pretty golden form, 'Aureum' is very ornamental and as vigorously self-sowing in habit as the green-leaved. The dwarf golden seed strain called 'Golden Moss' (to 15cm/6in) is frequently used as an edging plant for summer bedding schemes. Will grow almost anywhere, including dry, stony soil. Plant in autumn or spring and propagate by seed or division in spring. **Uses** Vile-tasting bitter herb that has recently proved effective for migraine and rheumatism. Never given to pregnant women. Fresh leaves may cause skin irritation or, if eaten, mouth ulcers.

**Horse-radish (*Armoracia rusticana*, Brassicaceae)** See Beningbrough Hall, p.64

**Hops (*Humulus lupulus*, Cannabaceae)** 3-6m (10-20ft). The twining stems and large, lobed, coarsely toothed leaves of this herbaceous climber are ideal for providing height in the herb garden, particularly in the golden-leaved form 'Aureus'. Plant in spring on moist, but well-drained soil and cut back dead top growth to the ground in early spring when new shoots appear. Propagate from softwood cuttings of female plants in spring. See Hardwick Hall, p.36. **Uses** Aside from the use of the flowers to flavour beer, hops are also a sedative herb, used by North American Indians as a painkiller and to treat insomnia, hence the use of the dried flowers in hop pillows which aid sleep, soothe the nerves and help relieve ear and toothache. Not suitable for those with a history of depression.

**Lovage (*Levisticum officinale*, Apiaceae)** See Hardwick Hall, p.40

**Mint (*Mentha* spp., Lamiaceae)** See Acorn Bank, p.14

**Soapwort (*Saponaria officinalis*, Caryophyllaceae)** See Hardwick Hall, p.37

**Salad Burnet (*Sanguisorba officinalis*, Rosaceae)** 30-100cm (1-3ft). An erect and graceful perennial, with a basal rosette of divided leaves, composed of small, neatly toothed individual leaflets giving the whole a rather lacy appearance. The tiny red bottle-brush flowers are produced at the tips of long, wiry stalks from mid-summer. Plant in autumn or spring into rich, moisture-retentive soil, preferably neutral to alkaline. Propagate by seed in autumn or spring or by division in spring. **Uses** A wound herb – hence its Latin name, *sanguis sorbere*, 'to soak up blood' – but the common name refers to its medieval use in salads. Used medicinally to treat haemorrhoids, burns and skin diseases. Use young leaves in green salads or add to soups, stews and cold summer drinks. Cut flowers back to renew the foliage.

**Self-heal (*Prunella vulgaris*, Lamiaceae)** See Acorn Bank, p.17

**Sweet Cicely (*Myrrhis odorata*, Apiaceae)** See Beningbrough Hall, p.63

**Tansy (*Tanacetum vulgare*, Asteraceae)** 0.6-1.2m (2-4ft). Pungent, invasive herb with feathery leaves and clusters of yellow, button-like flowers in late summer. Plant on any soil or divide in autumn or spring. **Uses** An aromatic strewing herb with insecticidal properties. Also used in a custard known as 'tansy' and to flavour tansy cakes and puddings. Medicinally used to treat menstrual complaints and to cure round or thread worms in children. It is so toxic that it is now rarely used internally and certainly never given to pregnant women.

**Valerian, All Heal (*Valeriana officinalis*, Valerianaceae)** 50-150cm (20-60in). Bright green, erect, perennial herb, quite distinct from the red valerian of gardens, *Centranthus ruber albus*. True valerian has long, divided leaves and clusters of pink flowers from June to August, but it is the short, rhizomatous root which is used medicinally. Plant in well-drained, but moisture-retentive, neutral to alkaline soil. Divide in spring or autumn or sow seed in spring. There are other ornamental valerians but only *V. officinalis* has powerful medicinal properties. **Uses** The dried roots have bitter, rather unpleasant smell and have been used since Classical times as a strong sedative and anti-depressant. Extracts are also used to flavour ice-cream, soft drinks, beers and tobacco.

## Shade

**Comfrey (*Symphytum officinale*, Boraginaceae)** See Gunby Hall, p.27 and Castle Drogo, p.71

**Lady's Mantle (*Alchemilla mollis*, Rosaceae)** See Acorn Bank, p.17

**Lemon Balm (*Melissa officinalis*, Lamiaceae)** See Springhill, p.46

**Lungwort (*Pulmonaria officinalis*, Boraginaceae)** To 30cm (12in). The long, hairy, white-spotted, semi-evergreen leaves of lungwort make a tolerant, spreading groundcover for dry shade. Produces small drooping spikes of pink and blue flowers in early spring. 'Sissinghurst White' is a particularly fine form with white flowers. Plant in autumn or spring on almost any soil, and divide at the same time to increase. **Uses** Closely associated with the sixteenth- and seventeenth-century 'Doctrine of Signatures' which theorised that herbs were given by God to cure human illness and that any plant whose parts resemble a human organ may be used to treat ill-health in that organ. The lung-shaped and spotted leaves were thought to resemble diseased lungs and were therefore used to treat coughs and bronchitis. The young leaves were also added to salads and soups and an extract of the plant is used in vermouth.

**Monkshood (*Aconitum napellus*, Ranunculaceae)**
To 90cm (36in). The superb spikes of blue, hooded flowers carried by tuberous-rooted monkshood are indispensable for late summer borders. Plant on moisture-retentive, but well-drained soil and divide in spring or autumn to increase. Sow fresh seed in autumn. **Uses** A pain-killer and sedative, but highly poisonous, even in minute doses. Used by qualified practioners to treat pleurisy, arthritis, neuralgia and heart failure. See also Acorn Bank, p.10

**Pennyroyal (*Mentha pulegium*, Lamiaceae)** See Acorn Bank, p.16

**Sweet Woodruff (*Galium odoratum*, Rubiaceae)**
18-45cm (6-18in). A gentle carpet of delicate stems clothed in star-like whorls of aromatic leaves and a froth of clustered white flowers in May and June characterise this sweetly scented herb, which makes a good groundcover plant for dappled shade. Plant in spring on well-drained, but moisture-retentive soil. Divide the creeping rhizome in spring or sow seed in autumn or spring. **Uses** Fresh leaves were used as poultices for cuts and wounds, to make a sedative tea, or in the treatment of liver and spleen disorders. Dried leaves smelling of fresh-cut hay were hung as scented garlands. Also soaked in white wine to make *Maitrank* or *Maibowle*, an Alsatian or German drink consumed on the first of May.

## Annuals, biennials, and marginally tender perennials

All annuals and biennials are easily grown from seed, but many are not well suited to pricking out or otherwise transplanting the young seedlings after germination. These (marked 'DS' below) should be sown straight into the open ground, or into small pots or cell modules where there will be no need to disturb the root systems. See Barrington Court, p.85, Hardwick Hall, p.38 and Sissinghurst, p.73 for more seed sowing tips. For cuttings of tender perennials, see Bateman's, p.22 and Hardwick Hall, p.40.

**Angelica (*Angelica archangelica*, Apiaceae)** See Acorn Bank, p.18

**Anise (*Pimpinella anisum*, Apiaceae)** Hardy annual, 10-50cm (4-20in). A lightly hairy plant with aniseed-flavoured foliage, becoming fine and almost carrot-like at the stem tips, and producing little umbels of white or pink flowers in late summer, followed by fruits with two hairy seeds to each capsule. DS Sow seed in spring in a well-drained soil in a sunny position. **Uses** Primarily grown for the culinary use of the seed in cakes and breads, although the foliage may also be added to soups and salads. Used in alchoholic drinks such as Pernod, Ouzo and Anisette. Also medicinally for gastric disorders and to relieve coughs and asthma. Seed ripens only after a hot summer. Harvest when the tips of the fruits are greenish-grey. Cut in bunches and hang upside down in a dry place to finish ripening. Then thresh, winnow and clean to remove the chaff before storing in an airtight, opaque container.

**Basil (*Ocimum basilicum*, Lamiaceae)** See Sissinghurst, p.76

**Borage (*Borago officinalis*, Boraginaceae)** Hardy annual, 30-60cm (1-2ft). Bright, drooping clusters of flowers clasped within hairy calyces bring a wonderful strong tint of blue to the herb garden and attract bees. Readily self-sows, but rarely in the right position! Transplant the seedlings to a more desirable site while still small. Likes a sunny position on light, well-drained soil. Sow in spring. **Uses** Believed from ancient times to dispel melancholy and induce euphoria, the young leaves, with their slight cucumber flavour, were once boiled and eaten as a pot herb or shredded into salads. Medicinally has been used to treat pulmonary complaints. The flowers, stripped of their hairy calyces, make a cheerful addition to green salads or Pimms.

**Caraway (*Carum carvi*, Apiaceae)** Hardy biennial, 25-100cm (10-36in). Feathery plant with thread-like leaves and umbels of tiny pink to white flowers in summer. Likes a moisture-retentive, well-drained soil in a sunny position. DS Sow spring to autumn, although in cold climates spring-sown seed may not ripen. **Uses** The ribbed seeds were used in Middle Eastern and Jewish cuisine thousands of years before its introduction to Europe in the thirteenth century and now flavour confectionery, bread and cheeses and are also used in *schnapps*. The leaves may be used in soups and salads, while the roots may be cooked as a vegetable. Medicinally for indigestion, stomach ulcers and laryngitis. Gather and dry seeds as for anise.

**Chervil (*Anthriscus cerefolium*, Apiaceae)** See Sissinghurst, p.77

**Clary, Muscatel Sage (*Salvia sclarea*, Lamiaceae)** Hardy biennial, to 100cm (40in). With wrinkled, velvety, rather heart-shaped leaves typical of the sage family, clary produces erect, branching spikes of bi-coloured cream and lilac-blue flowers in spring and summer, and is particularly decorative in the form *S. sclarea* var. *turkestanica* with large, colourful bracts

Foxgloves (*Digitalis officinalis*)

of pink or white and pink stems. Likes full sun on well-drained to dry soil. Sow seed from spring to early autumn. **Uses** The common name may derive from the Latin verb 'to clear', due to its use in eye washes, but clary is also used medicinally as a digestive aid, but never given to pregnant women.

**Coriander (***Coriandrum sativum***, Apiaceae)** See Sissinghurst, p.77

**Dill (***Anethum graveolens***, Apiaceae)** See Sissinghurst, p.78

**Evening Primrose (***Oenothera biennis***, Onagraceae)** See Gunby Hall, p.28

**Fenugreek (***Trigonella foenum-graecum***, Papilionaceae)** Hardy annual, to 60cm (24in). Has the typical thrice-divided leaves of the pea family and small yellowish-white pea flowers in summer, tinged violet at the base, followed by the yellow-brown seeds for which the plant is most frequently grown. Prefers a sunny position on fertile, well-drained soil. Sow seed in spring. **Uses** The seeds are an important ingredient in curry powder and mango chutney, while the leaves are chopped and added to many Middle Eastern, Mediterranean and Indian dishes. Used medicinally to treat late-onset diabetes, and painful menstruation, but never given to pregnant women. Saponins from the plant are extracted for modern use in oral contraceptives. The seeds take about four months to mature, so early spring or autumn sowing is essential for a crop.

**Foxglove (***Digitalis officinalis***, Scrophulariaceae)** Hardy biennial or short-lived perennial, to 1m (3ft) with drooping spikes of glove-shaped purple, white or creamy flowers. Grows on moisture-retentive, neutral to acid soil in dappled or part-day shade and self-sows freely. Sow seed from early to late summer. **Uses** Extremely poisonous but also the source of digitalin, used in the treatment of heart disease. All species of *Digitalis* are toxic if eaten.

**French Tarragon (***Artemisia dracunculus***, Asteraceae)** See Hardwick Hall, p.37

**Lemon Verbena (***Aloysia triphylla***, Verbenaceae)** See Buckland Abbey, p.55

**Marjoram, Knotted or Sweet (***Origanum majorana***, Lamiaceae)** See Gunby Hall, p.31

**Nasturtium (***Tropaeolum majus***, Brassicaceae)** Hardy, trailing or climbing annual or short-lived perennial, to between 15cm (6in) and 2m (6ft) tall.

Likes sun or part-day shade and virtually any soil – the poorer the better, since rich soil encourages leaf growth rather than flowers. Sow seed in spring or autumn. **Uses** With pungent, peppery flowers, leaves and seeds, nasturtium is high in vitamin C and was thought to be effective against scurvy and respiratory infections. Also recommended for healthy skin, hair and eyes. Tear up flowers or use young leaves in salads. Chop young leaves for flavouring cheese and egg dishes. Pick flowerbuds for pickling as a caper substitute in May or early June.

**Parsley (***Petroselinum crispum***, Apiaceae)** See Barrington Court, p.85

**Pineapple Sage (***Salvia elegans* 'Scarlet Pineapple'**, Lamiaceae)** See Bateman's, p.21

**Pot Marigold (***Calendula officinalis***, Asteraceae)** Hardy annual, to 45cm (18in). Cheerful orange flowers which can brighten the garden right through the autumn until the first frosts. May survive a mild winter. Prefers a sunny position on well-drained soil. Sow seed in spring or autumn. **Uses** In the Middle Ages the flowers of calendula were a popular medicinal, culinary and cosmetic herb, used for intestinal and liver problems, and to heal all manner of skin complaints including warts and acne. Calendula petals were also dried for use in winter broths and the fresh flowers yielded a yellow dye, for colouring cheese and butter. Not given during pregnancy, but still used in herbal medicine particularly for skin problems.

**Summer Savory (***Satureja hortensis***, Lamiaceae)** See Sissinghurst, p.78

**Woad (***Isatis tinctoria***, Brassicaceae)** Hardy biennial or short-lived perennial, 0·5-1·2m (1½-4ft). Julius Caesar reported that the ancient Britons painted their bodies a bright blue with the dye extracted from the narrow leaves of this tap-rooted plant. Produces dense, branching heads of yellow flowers resembling rape in the second summer after germination, followed by large black seeds. Grow in rich, well-drained, neutral to alkaline soil in full sun. DS Sow in spring. **Uses** A popular dye plant until the seventeenth century, it was also used as a medicinal herb, particularly in ointments to treat ulcers, skin inflammation and to stop bleeding. Said to be anti-viral in action, it has been used in the treatment of meningitis, encephalitis, mumps and influenza and may have some anti-cancer effect.

# Gazetteer

## Addresses

**Acorn Bank**
Temple Sowerby, nr Penrith, Cumbria CA10 1SP

**Barrington Court**
Barrington, nr Illminster, Somerset TA19 0NQ

**Bateman's**
Burwash, Etchingham, East Sussex TN19 7DS

**Beningbrough Hall**
Beningbrough, York YO30 1DD

**Buckland Abbey**
Yelverton, Devon PL20 6EY

**Castle Drogo**
Drewsteignton, nr Exeter, Devon EX6 6PB

**Gunby Hall**
Gunby, nr Spilsby, Lincolnshire PE23 5SS

**Hardwick Hall**
Doe Lea, Chesterfield, Derbyshire S44 5QJ

**Sissinghurst Castle Garden**
Sissinghurst, nr Cranbrook, Kent TN17 2AB

**Springhill**
20 Springhill Road, Moneymore,
Magherafelt, Co. Londonderry BT45 7NQ

## Other National Trust Herb Gardens to visit

**Baddesley Clinton**
Rising Lane, Baddesley Clinton Village,
Knowle, Solihull, Warwickshire B93 0DQ

**Benthall Hall**
Broseley, Shropshire TF12 5RX

**Clumber Park**
The Estate Office, Clumber Park, Worksop,
Nottinghamshire S80 3AZ

**East Riddlesden Hall**
Bradford Road, Keighley, Yorkshire BD20 5EL

**Fenton House**
Windmill Hill, Hampstead, London NW3 6RT

**Hardy's Cottage**
Higher Brockhampton, nr Dorchester,
Dorset DT2 8QJ

**Ightham Mote**
Ivy Hatch, Sevenoaks, Kent TN15 0NT

**Knole**
Sevenoaks, Kent TN15 0RP

**Lamb House**
West Street, Rye, East Sussex TN31 7ES

**Little Moreton Hall**
Congleton, Cheshire CW12 4SD

**Melford Hall**
Long Melford, Sudbury, Suffolk CO10 9AH

**Moseley Old Hall**
Moseley Old Hall Lane, Fordhouses
Wolverhampton, Staffordshire WV10 7HY

**Quarry Bank Mill**
Wilmslow, Cheshire SK9 4LA

**St Michael's Mount**
Marazion, nr Penzance, Cornwall TR17 0EF

**Scotney Castle Garden**
Lamberhurst, Tunbridge Wells, Kent TN3 8JN

**Snowshill Manor**
Snowshill, nr Broadway, Gloucestershire WR12 7JU

**Wordsworth House**
Main Street, Cockermouth, Cumbria CA13 9RX

# Index